# 5 WAYS WITH...

# 5 WAYS WITH...

TAKE **ONE** KEY INGREDIENT AND CREATE

**FIVE** FANTASTIC FAMILY MEALS

## CHRISTELLE LE RU

**HarperCollins**_Publishers_

To Noémie, Éloïse, Yohann & Émeric,
with love from Mum

## By the same author

*Simply Irresistible French Desserts* (2005)

*French Fare* (2006)

*Passion Chocolat* (2007)

*Fresh Start* (2008)

*Self-Publish!* (2009)

National Library of New Zealand Cataloguing-in-Publication Data

Le Ru, Christelle, 1975-
Five ways with— / Christelle Le Ru.
Includes index.
ISBN 978-1-86950-859-3
1. Cookery. I. Title.
641.5—dc 22

First published 2010
HarperCollins*Publishers* (New Zealand) Limited
PO Box 1, Shortland Street, Auckland 1140

ISBN 978 1 86950 818 0

Cover design by Christa Moffitt, Christabella Designs
Cover image by Nicky Kerr
Typesetting by IslandBridge

Produced by Phoenix, on 128gsm Matt Art
Printed in China

# Contents

# Introduction

Dear Readers,

As a busy working mum to four preschoolers, I used to have the same problem as everyone else when dinner time comes. The same question inevitably came up day after day — 'What on earth am I going to cook tonight to feed my tribe?' This is when the idea of cooking meals using basic, inexpensive and nutritious ingredients while preparing them in different and interesting ways occurred to me, and this is how I ended up writing *Five Ways With . . .*

What I like most about the recipes in this book is that the ingredients I have used are pantry must-haves and other commonly used foods. These days I find that my typical daily routine consists of rushing like a mad woman with a baby on one arm while trying to get as much work done as possible and making sure the other three children are all still in one piece by bedtime. Like many people leading a busy life, I find I hardly have a minute to stop and catch my breath, let alone give some forethought to dinner. This is why in *Five Ways With . . .* there's always bound to be an appetizing dish that can be cooked without too much planning (or blowing the budget), and using whatever happens to be on hand.

Often one ingredient may be substituted for another you like better or simply have in stock. I always like to encourage people to use my recipes as a helpful tool rather than as a strict guideline of what should be done and not done. While I think recipes are very useful and can provide lots of new, innovative ideas, it is also nice to add your own personal touch to them. When it comes to cooking, I believe letting your creativity loose is the key!

As you will see, my food looks very much like dishes anyone can make. This is the whole idea. I do not wish to show dishes so perfect that they look unattainable! On the contrary, my point is to try to make people realize how easy it can be to cook healthy, delicious and inexpensive dishes that don't require hours of slaving over the stove (or formal training, for that matter).

I'm sure that once you have tasted some of the delicious homemade dishes presented in this book, takeaways ordered out of desperation (and lack of dinner ideas) will suddenly seem less appealing. And since the dishes also focus on both the cost and nutritional value of the ingredients they are made from, this will be beneficial to your health as well as your wallet! So what are you waiting for? Get cooking and enjoy the result!

*Christelle*

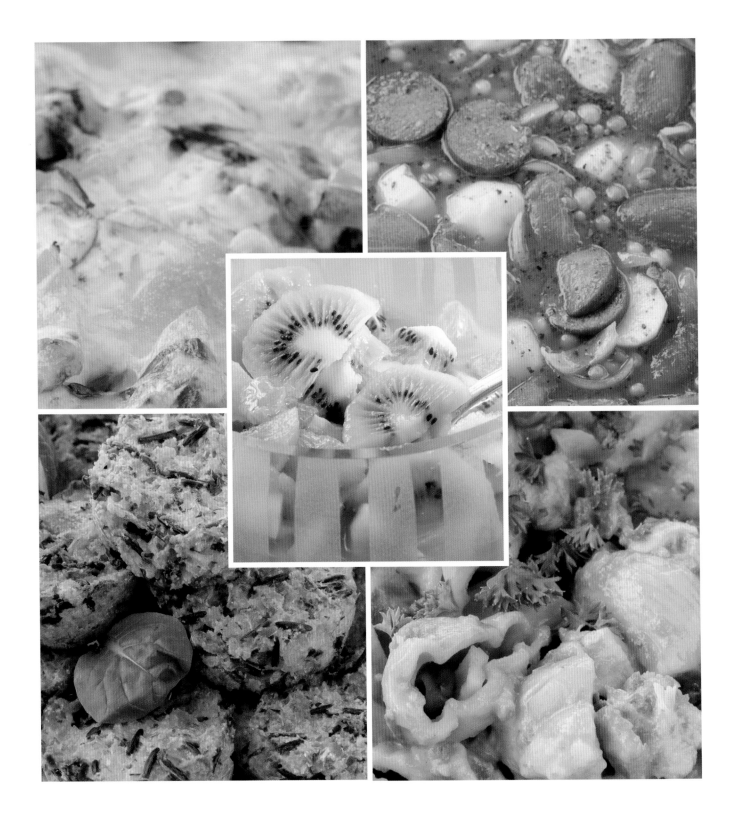

# Broccoli

Broccoli and
fish gratin

Broccoli and
shrimp tartlets

Broccoli
terrine

Vegetarian
broccoli curry

Creamy broccoli and
cauliflower soup

The cultivation of broccoli originates in Italy. Its texture ranges from a fibrous and crunchy stalk to a soft floret. Don't be put off by the distinctive smell of the sulphurous compounds that are released while cooking broccoli as it is one of the most nutritious vegetables.

Like other cruciferous vegetables (eg, cabbage, cauliflower and Brussels sprouts), broccoli contains multiple nutrients that have been shown to have potent anti-cancer properties. Broccoli also contains significant amounts of calcium, vitamin C, vitamin K, vitamin A, folate and dietary fibre. In other words, it truly deserves being called a super-food. It is not only inexpensive and nutritious, it also tastes good. If regularly included in your diet, it can help improve and maintain your health.

When selecting broccoli, look for floret clusters that are compact and uniformly green in colour with no yellowing. The stalk and stems should be firm.

Broccoli will keep for up to a week in the fridge; however, it is best eaten within a couple of days. It can also be blanched and frozen for up to a year. Broccoli is usually prepared steamed or stir-fried but may be eaten raw. Bear in mind that the way you cook your vegetables dramatically affects the amount of nutrients they impart. Steaming is a good way to cook broccoli, whereas boiling causes a greater loss of nutrients.

# Broccoli and fish gratin

*Serves 6*

There is nothing like a gratin to warm up a cold winter's day. Comfort food *par excellence*, gratins can be made with almost any ingredient you happen to have on hand. The flavours of this gratin are enhanced by the cheese sauce, which can be spiced up with a small amount of curry powder or a pinch of cayenne if desired.

4 large potatoes

600g white fish fillets, such as red cod

1 tablespoon extra-virgin olive oil

2 broccoli heads

## Cheese sauce

55g butter

2 heaped tablespoons flour

1 egg

600ml milk

55ml fresh cream

1 teaspoon dried thyme

1 teaspoon dried tarragon

salt and pepper

100g tasty Cheddar cheese, grated

Preheat the oven to 180°C (350°F) fan bake. Grease a large, deep oven dish.

Peel and finely slice the potatoes. Place them at the bottom of the prepared dish. Brush the fish fillets with the olive oil and use to cover the potatoes. Cut the broccoli florets into bite-size pieces and scatter over the fish.

To make the cheese sauce, melt the butter in a large saucepan. Remove from the heat and mix in the flour to make a thick paste. Beat in the egg. Stir in the milk and the fresh cream gradually to avoid lumps. Add the thyme and tarragon, and season with salt and pepper. Cook over a low heat for 10 to 15 minutes, stirring continuously, until the sauce thickens. Mix in the grated Cheddar cheese and pour over the fish and vegetables.

Bake in the oven for 45 minutes, or until the potatoes are tender and the topping is golden. Leave to sit for 5 minutes before serving with some crusty bread or toast.

# Broccoli and shrimp tartlets

*Serves 8*

These savoury tartlets are fun to make and delicious to eat. They are suitable for a light lunch or a buffet party, or to take along on a picnic.

## Shortcrust pastry

1 egg

125g butter, melted

100g wholemeal flour

125g white flour

## Filling

1 broccoli head

100g shrimps, peeled

1 tablespoon olive oil

4 eggs

55g feta cheese

freshly ground pepper

Preheat the oven to 200°C (400°F) fan bake. Grease 8 individual tartlet baking tins.

To make the shortcrust pastry, mix the egg with the melted butter. Add the flours and mix well. Divide the pastry into 8 portions and press with your fingers into the base and sides of the prepared tins. Prick all over with a fork and chill for 15 minutes.

To make the filling, clean the broccoli head and cook the florets in a steamer for 5 minutes. Cut the florets into smaller pieces. Place the shrimps in a frying pan with the oil, and cook over a medium heat for a few minutes. Break the eggs into a bowl and beat with a fork. Crumble the feta cheese and add to the eggs, along with the steamed broccoli florets and shrimps. Season with freshly ground pepper.

Bake the pastry shells for 5 to 10 minutes, until crispy and slightly golden. Lower the oven temperature to 180°C (350°F). Fill the pastry shells with the egg mixture and bake for another 20 minutes or until just set. Enjoy warm or cold.

# Broccoli terrine

*Serves 6*

This dish makes a refreshing starter or a light lunch. Very simple to make and quick to prepare — you can't get it wrong. Depending on the season, you may wish to substitute other suitable seasonal vegetables for the broccoli and carrots.

## Tip

Using the *bain-marie* technique when baking an egg-based dish is a good way to stop the mixture from curdling. To ensure a creamy texture, care should be taken to cook the dish at the correct temperature for the specified time.

2 carrots

1 broccoli head

6 eggs

200g natural yoghurt

1 teaspoon ground cumin

salt and pepper

Preheat the oven to 180°C (350°F) fan bake. Grease a 23 × 12cm (9 × 5 inch) loaf tin.

Peel the carrots and slice lengthways. Clean the broccoli head and cut off the stalk. Cook the broccoli florets along with the carrot sticks in a steamer for 5 minutes or until tender.

Combine the eggs and yoghurt in a food processor. Season with the ground cumin, salt and pepper. Transfer to a bowl and fold in the broccoli florets and carrot sticks.

Pour this mixture into the prepared tin and place into a larger ovenproof dish partly filled with water (*bain-marie*), so that the water comes about half-way up the sides of the loaf tin. Bake for 40 minutes or until the terrine is just set.

Remove from the oven and leave the tin until cool. Once cool, the terrine can be turned over delicately and transferred to a serving dish. Cut into slices and serve with a few spoonfuls of tomato salsa or mayonnaise on the side.

# Vegetarian broccoli curry

*Serves 6*

Curries are versatile and loved by almost everyone. Typical of Indian cuisine, they have become very popular in many other parts of the world. This recipe results in a mild-to medium-strength dish, but you can easily spice it up to suit your own palate.

2 potatoes

2 broccoli heads

1 onion

1 tablespoon oil

1 tablespoon ground ginger

2 tablespoons tikka masala paste

450ml water

3 tomatoes

salt and pepper

Peel the potatoes and cut into chunks. Cook in a steamer for 15 minutes. Clean the broccoli heads and cut off the stalks. Cook the florets in a steamer for 5 minutes or until tender.

Peel and slice the onion. Place in a frying pan with the oil and ground ginger. Fry over a high heat for a couple of minutes while stirring. Add the tikka masala paste and water, and mix well. Cover and simmer over a low heat for 15 minutes.

Place the tomatoes in a bowl and cover with boiling water for 30 seconds to make them easy to peel. Remove the skin and seeds, and roughly chop the flesh. Add to the curry mixture with the steamed vegetables and cook, uncovered, for another 10 minutes. Season with salt and pepper.

Serve with basmati or long-grain rice, a dollop of natural yoghurt and some naan bread.

# Creamy broccoli and cauliflower soup

*Serves 6*

---

Nothing chases the cold away like a hearty, homemade soup. This broccoli and cauliflower soup is both creamy and tasty, with all the nutritional benefits provided by these vegetable super-foods.

2 potatoes

1 cauliflower

750ml milk

250ml fresh cream

250ml water

100g cheese, grated

1 pinch cayenne pepper

salt and pepper

1 broccoli head

Peel the potatoes and cut into chunks. Cut the cauliflower into 4 pieces, removing the end of the stalk. Place these vegetables in a steamer and cook for 10 minutes or until tender.

Transfer to a food processor and blend, adding the milk gradually. Add the fresh cream and water, and mix well. Mix in the grated cheese. Season with cayenne pepper, salt and pepper. Pour this mixture into a large saucepan, bring to a simmer, and cook over a low heat for 20 minutes, stirring occasionally.

Clean the broccoli head and cut off the stalk. Cook florets in a steamer for 5 minutes or until tender. Delicately fold the broccoli florets into the cauliflower mixture (saving some to place on top for decoration), simmer for a further 10 minutes, and serve with some crispy bread.

# Cabbage

Cabbage
gratin

Little cabbage
flans

Stuffed cabbage
leaves

Cabbage and chicken
casserole

Cabbage
soup

Cabbage is inexpensive and has been a dietary staple throughout the world for many centuries. In France, cabbage soup is a classic dish which even lends its name to a famous movie, *La Soupe au Chou*.

Cabbage is widely cultivated and keeps well. This makes it available virtually all year round, although it is at its best during late autumn and the winter months. Like broccoli, it is a crucifer with well-known cancer-fighting properties and is an excellent source of vitamin C.

Try to select a firm and dense cabbage with shiny, crisp leaves. Avoid buying it halved or shredded, as once it is cut its vitamin C content rapidly degrades. Cabbage will keep for a week in the fridge but needs to be used quickly once cut.

To prepare cabbage, remove and discard the thick, fibrous outer leaves. Cut shortly before cooking and remember that overcooking cabbage can result in an unpleasant odour.

To cut the cabbage into smaller pieces, first quarter it and remove the core. The quarters may be cut into chunks of various sizes or shredded in a food processor. Cabbage can be eaten raw, braised, boiled, steamed, sautéed, stir-fried or microwaved.

# Stuffed cabbage leaves

*Serves 6*

While cabbage may not be the most appealing vegetable to many, it can be used in many ways. In this recipe, take advantage of the large cabbage leaves to wrap up your meat leftovers. Once mixed with a few vegetables and seasoned properly, these leftovers will provide an unusual and nutritious dish at a very low cost.

1 cabbage

**Filling**

2 slices wholemeal bread

100ml milk, tepid

200g cooked leftover meat

1 onion

2 cloves garlic

2 carrots

1 bunch fresh parsley

30g butter

2 egg yolks

**Sauce**

500ml water

3 tablespoons chicken stock powder

1 × 140g tin tomato paste

Preheat the oven to 180°C (350°F) fan bake. Grease a deep 35 × 27cm (14 × 11 inch) oven dish.

Place the bread, with crusts removed, in a bowl. Pour the tepid milk over the bread and set aside. Mince the leftover meat.

Peel the onion, garlic and carrots. Grate the carrots and chop the onion and garlic. Wash and dry the parsley and finely chop. Place these ingredients in a frying pan with the butter, and cook over a medium heat for 10 minutes while stirring.

Transfer to a mixing bowl and blend in the egg yolks. Add the milk and bread and the minced leftover meat. Divide into 6 portions.

Bring some water to the boil in a large saucepan. Remove the largest outer leaves of the cabbage and choose 6 blemish-free leaves. Put them in the boiling water for 5 minutes.

Remove from the saucepan and dry. Place a leaf on a plate and spoon one portion of the filling into the centre. Roll the cabbage leaf into the shape of a ball and transfer to the prepared dish. Repeat until all the filling and the prepared cabbage leaves have been used up.

To make the sauce, bring the water to the boil and add the chicken stock powder. Gradually pour the stock over the tomato paste in a bowl and mix well. Pour this sauce over the stuffed cabbage leaves and bake for 45 minutes.

# Cabbage gratin

*Serves 6*

Simple to prepare, a gratin always makes a delicious dinner. Serve it with a green salad and some freshly baked bread for a wholesome meal.

½ cabbage

55g butter

200g ham

salt and pepper

## Cheese sauce

55g butter

2 heaped tablespoons flour

2 tablespoons sour cream

1 egg

600ml milk

salt and pepper

1 teaspoon dried mixed herbs

100g cheese, grated

Preheat the oven to 180°C (350°F) fan bake. Grease a medium-size, deep ovenproof dish.

To make the cheese sauce, melt the butter in a pan. Remove from the heat and mix in the flour, sour cream and egg. Gradually stir in the milk. Season with salt and pepper, and add the mixed herbs. Cook over a low heat until the sauce thickens. Stir in the grated cheese. Set aside.

Remove and discard the outer cabbage leaves. Remove the tough stalks on the remaining leaves and cook in a large saucepan of boiling salted water for 10 minutes. Drain and shred the leaves.

Place the shredded leaves in a frying pan with the butter. Add the diced ham and season with salt and pepper. Cook over a medium heat for 10 minutes, stirring occasionally. Spread a layer of the cabbage mixture on the bottom of the prepared dish and cover with some cheese sauce. Repeat, until all the cabbage mixture and cheese sauce have been used up, finishing with a layer of cheese sauce. Bake for 35 minutes or until the top is golden. Serve hot, sprinkled with mixed herbs and with a green salad on the side.

# Cabbage and chicken casserole

## Serves 4

The delicious flavour of thyme gives this recipe a Mediterranean touch. This casserole may be prepared a day ahead and reheated in a large saucepan, and, as with most casseroles, the flavours will develop with time. Any leftovers can be frozen.

2 tablespoons fresh thyme

2 tablespoons extra-virgin olive oil

2 chicken breasts, boneless and skinless

2 chicken thighs

1 cabbage

2 onions

2 rashers bacon, chopped

55g butter

2 cloves garlic

salt and pepper

1 tablespoon chicken stock powder

300ml boiling water

Mix half the thyme with the olive oil and use to brush the chicken breasts and thighs.

Remove the outer cabbage leaves and the tough base. Cut the cabbage into quarters and cook in a large saucepan filled with boiling salted water for 5 minutes. Drain and shred the cabbage, taking the stalk off the largest leaves.

Peel and slice the onions and place in a frying pan, along with the bacon and butter. Cook for a few minutes over a medium heat. Add the shredded cabbage, peeled and crushed garlic, and remaining thyme to the pan. Season with salt and pepper.

Place the chicken breasts and thighs in a large saucepan and cover with the cabbage mixture. Mix the chicken stock powder with the boiling water and pour over the chicken and vegetables. Cover and cook over a low heat for an hour, stirring occasionally. Transfer to a serving dish and serve accompanied by boiled potatoes and Dijon mustard.

# Little cabbage flans

*Serves 6*

A flan is a type of baked dish containing a mixture of eggs, milk and flour plus some additional ingredients. These ingredients will vary, depending on your taste and whether you choose to make a sweet flan or a savoury flan. This version, making use of cabbage leaves, is light and tasty. Flans may be eaten warm or cold.

½ cabbage

2 onions

2 cloves garlic

30g butter

4 eggs

250ml milk

## Cheese sauce

30g butter

1 heaped tablespoon flour

1 tablespoon sour cream

1 egg

300ml milk

salt and pepper

100g cheese, grated

Preheat the oven to 180°C (350°F) fan bake. Grease a mini-muffin tin.

Wash the cabbage and remove the tough stalk at the base. Cut into chunks and cook for 10 minutes in a large saucepan filled with salted boiling water. Remove from the water and drain. Place in a food processor and purée.

Peel and finely chop the onions and garlic. Place in a frying pan with the butter and cook over a medium to high heat for a few minutes. Mix in the puréed cabbage.

To make the cheese sauce, melt the butter in a pan. Remove from the heat and mix in the flour, sour cream and egg. Gradually stir in the milk. Season with salt and pepper. Cook over a low heat until the sauce thickens. Stir in the grated cheese.

Transfer the cheese sauce to a bowl and add the cabbage mixture. Beat in the eggs. Gradually mix in the milk.

Pour this mixture into the prepared tin and bake for 25 minutes or until set. Remove from the oven and leave to cool. Repeat to use up the flan mixture. Transfer the flans to a serving plate, sprinkle with some freshly chopped chives, and serve warm with a tomato-based dip.

# Cabbage soup

*Serves 8*

Cabbage soup is a traditional dish in France, where it is very popular in rural areas. There are many different recipes for it — here is my own favourite version.

100g shoulder bacon

1 onion

1 leek

30g butter

5 carrots

½ a bunch of celery

½ cabbage (500g)

2 tablespoons fresh parsley

salt and freshly ground pepper

3l water

Chop the bacon into small pieces. Peel and slice the onion. Wash the leek and finely chop the white and pale green parts. Place in a frying pan with the butter and cook over a medium heat for a few minutes until tender.

Peel and slice the carrots. Wash the celery and finely chop. Wash and roughly cut the cabbage into bite-size pieces. Wash and finely chop the parsley.

Place all the ingredients in a pressure cooker, and season with salt and freshly ground pepper. Add the water, tightly close the lid, and cook for 20 minutes.

Let the steam out and remove the lid. Transfer to a serving dish and enjoy hot with some cheese toasties.

# Onions

Onion
soup

Onion and
chicken casserole

Onion
tart

Stuffed
onions

Onion and
tomato gratin

Onions may make you cry and your breath smell, but they will most likely also delight your taste buds. Used in virtually every type of cuisine, onions are available year-round. Native to Asia and the Middle East, they have been cultivated for thousands of years. These days, onions come fresh, frozen, canned, pickled, powdered, chopped and dehydrated. There are brown, red and white onions, brown being the most popular.

The sulphurous compounds found in onions and garlic produce their pungent odour and health benefits. Eating onions can lower cholesterol levels and blood pressure, because they are a rich source of chromium and vitamin C.

There are two main categories of onions: spring/summer fresh onions and autumn/winter storage onions. The former have thin, light-coloured skin, and are typically sweeter and milder than storage onions. Fresh onions are ideal for salads and lightly cooked dishes, while storage onions are best for dishes that require longer cooking times and more flavour.

Look for onions that are clean and well-shaped, with crisp and dry outer skins. Avoid those that are sprouting or show signs of mould. Store onions at room temperature, away from bright light, and in a manner that ensures they are well ventilated. To stop the juice from irritating your eyes when cutting onions, try chilling the onions for an hour or so before cutting them, or cut them under running water. If you still find it unbearable, consider wearing goggles (seriously!).

# Stuffed onions

*Serves 6*

This inexpensive recipe is a very humble way to cook onions. If you have any meat leftovers, they can be used in place of the eggs to make the filling.

3 eggs

½ bunch fresh parsley

6 large onions

3 tablespoons mayonnaise

salt and pepper

1 avocado

55g cheese, grated

Preheat the oven to 180°C (350°F) fan bake. Grease a deep 35 × 27cm (14 × 11 inch) rectangular oven dish.

Place the eggs in a saucepan filled with water, and cook for 10 minutes once the water starts boiling. Remove the eggs from the water and leave to cool.

Wash the parsley. Peel the onions, cut the top off each one, then place it back on. Cook in a steamer for 10 minutes. Remove the inner flesh of the onions, discard half of it (or use in another recipe) and place the rest in a food processor with the parsley.

Blend the parsley and the onion flesh, then mix in half the mayonnaise and season with salt and pepper. Remove the flesh from the avocado and cut into small pieces. Add to the onion mixture and set aside.

Peel the hard-boiled eggs. Place in a bowl and crumble, mixing in the remaining mayonnaise and grated cheese.

To assemble, place the onion shells in the prepared dish. Fill with the parsley mixture and top with the egg mixture. Cover each onion with its lid and bake for 15 minutes. Serve hot.

# Onion soup

*Serves 6*

Onion soup is a classic dish, and although the task of peeling and chopping a large number of onions is unenviable, the result is definitely worth it.

8 onions

55g butter

30g flour

1¼l water

2 tablespoons chicken stock powder

salt and pepper

100g croûtons

200g cheese, grated

Peel and finely chop the onions. Place in a frying pan with the butter, and cook over a medium heat for 10 minutes or until golden. Sprinkle with the flour and mix well while cooking for a few more minutes.

Bring the water to the boil and mix in the chicken stock powder. Gradually pour the stock over the onions. Season with salt and pepper. Cover and cook over a low heat for an hour.

Adjust the seasoning if necessary, and serve hot with croûtons and grated cheese on top.

# Onion tart

*Serves 6*

This is a delicious way to use up any onions left in your pantry. This tart is best served warm with a green salad, but it may also be eaten cold in a packed lunch. It will keep for a few days in the fridge.

150g puff pastry

6 onions

30g butter

100g ham

2 eggs

3 tablespoons flour

3 tablespoons sour cream

salt and pepper, to taste

Preheat the oven to 200°C (400°F) fan bake. Grease a 23cm (9 inch) round baking tin.

Roll out the puff pastry and press it with your fingers into the base and sides of the prepared tin. Prick all over with a fork and chill for 15 minutes.

Peel and finely chop the onions. Place in a frying pan with the butter and cook over a medium heat for 10 minutes or until golden. Transfer to a mixing bowl.

Dice the ham and add to the onions. Beat in the eggs, flour and sour cream. Season with salt and pepper.

Bake the pastry shell for 10 minutes. Lower the oven temperature to 180°C (350°F). Pour the onion filling into the pastry shell and bake for 30 minutes or until golden.

# Onion and chicken casserole

*Serves 4*

The cranberry sauce gives this casserole a sweet taste, while the wine vinegar and pickled onions have a rather sour flavour. This dish can be made ahead of time and reheated or frozen for convenience.

2 chicken thighs

2 chicken breasts, boneless and skinless

55g butter

1 x 500g jar pickled onions

150g bacon, diced

2 tablespoons dried thyme

330ml beer

salt and pepper

2 tablespoons cranberry sauce

1 tablespoon wine vinegar

Place the chicken thighs and breasts into a frying pan with half the butter. Cook over a high heat for a few minutes on all sides until golden. Remove from the pan and set aside.

Drain the pickled onions and place in the frying pan with the diced bacon. Cook over a high heat for a few minutes. Return the chicken to the pan and sprinkle with the thyme. Pour the beer over the meat, and season with salt and pepper.

Cover and simmer for an hour, stirring once in a while. Mix in the cranberry sauce and wine vinegar. Simmer for a further 15 minutes. Serve hot with steamed rice or pasta.

# Onion and tomato gratin

*Serves 4*

Indulge yourself with this unusual gratin. The onions, once cooked and combined with the other ingredients, take on a sweet taste that will have you coming back for more.

4 eggs

4 onions

30g butter

100ml white wine

salt and pepper

70g tomato paste

100g sour cream

150g cheese, grated

Preheat the oven to 200°C (400°F) fan bake. Grease a 20cm (8 inch) round oven dish.

Place the eggs in a saucepan filled with water, and cook for 10 minutes once the water starts boiling. Remove the eggs from the water and leave to cool.

Peel and slice the onions and place in a frying pan with the butter. Once tender and slightly golden pour in the wine. Season with salt and pepper, and mix in the tomato paste. Cook uncovered over a low heat until approximately half the liquid has evaporated. Mix in the sour cream and half of the grated cheese.

Spread this mixture into the prepared tin. Peel and slice the hard-boiled eggs. Cover the onion mixture with sliced eggs and the remaining grated cheese. Bake for 10 to 15 minutes, or until the cheese has melted. Sprinkle with freshly ground pepper and serve hot with a green salad on the side.

# Potatoes

Potato and
omelette gratin

Potato and
bacon cakes

Potato and
smoked fish stew

Chicken and
potato soup

Potato and
fish mash

Whatever their form, potatoes are comfort food. The world's number-one vegetable crop originated in South America and now comes in many different varieties, which vary in size, shape, colour, texture, starch content and flavour. Waxy potatoes' high water content make them good for boiling, salads and casseroles; whereas floury potatoes are best for mashing, wedges, roasting, baking and chips. Varieties like Desiree or Red Ruby are general-purpose potatoes.

Potatoes' neutral, starchy flavour makes them a good complement to many dishes. Best known for their carbohydrate content and as a high-energy food, they are a surprisingly rich source of nutrients. Their skin is a concentrated source of fibre, so it's best to consume both the flesh and the skin. Simply scrub off any dirt.

Virtually fat-free, potatoes are a good source of vitamins C and B6, are rich in minerals, particularly potassium, but low in sodium. Note that the cooking method (such as frying in oil) and the variety of the potato can significantly vary the nutritional content and glycemic index (GI).

Choose potatoes that are firm, relatively smooth and free of decay. They should not be sprouting or have the green coloration that can indicate a toxic alkaloid which develops when potatoes are exposed to sunlight. Store in a paper bag in a cool, dark place to avoid premature sprouting. Clean and cut directly before cooking to avoid the discoloration that occurs with exposure to air.

# Potato and smoked fish stew

*Serves 6*

This stew contains just the right balance of nutrients and should be enjoyed without guilt. The garlic mayonnaise may be replaced with regular mayonnaise; however, the garlic flavour goes particularly well with fish.

2 leeks

5 carrots

500g waxy potatoes

1 celery stalk

1 onion

3 whole cloves

1 bay leaf

1 teaspoon dried mixed herbs

salt and pepper

500ml milk

500ml water

800g smoked fish fillets

2 lemons

## Garlic mayonnaise

1 egg yolk

1 tablespoon Dijon mustard

200ml vegetable oil

3 cloves garlic

½ teaspoon dried parsley

To make the garlic mayonnaise, whip the egg yolk with the mustard, and gradually pour the vegetable oil into it. Make sure to add the oil very slowly to start with so that the egg yolk and oil are completely blended together before adding the remaining oil. Mix in the peeled and crushed garlic cloves and finely chopped parsley.

Wash the leeks. Cut the white and pale green part into three pieces. Peel the carrots and slice lengthways into sticks. Peel the potatoes and cut into chunks. Wash the celery and slice lengthways into sticks, approximately 5cm (2 inches) long. Peel the onion and stick the whole cloves into its flesh.

Place all these vegetables along with the bay leaf and dried mixed herbs into a large saucepan filled with boiling water. Season with salt and pepper. Cook for 20 minutes from the moment the water starts boiling again.

Pour the milk and the water into a saucepan. Bring to the boil and turn off the heat. Place the smoked fish into the liquid and soak for 10 minutes.

Drain the fish and vegetables and transfer to a serving dish. Sprinkle with the juice of a lemon. Serve with a spoonful of garlic mayonnaise, a few lemon slices, and some crusty bread.

# Potato and omelette gratin

*Serves 6*

This gratin will soon become a family favourite. It will be much appreciated on a cool evening, and may be served on its own or with a side salad.

30g butter

1 clove garlic

6 eggs

200ml milk

150ml fresh cream

salt and pepper

8 potatoes

100g tasty Cheddar cheese, grated

Preheat the oven to 180°C (350°F) fan bake. Grease a deep 35 × 27cm (14 × 11 inch) rectangular oven dish with the butter. Peel the garlic and use to rub the bottom and sides of the dish.

Mix the eggs, milk and fresh cream together in a bowl. Season with salt and pepper.

Peel and slice the potatoes. Place a third of the potatoes at the bottom of the prepared dish, and top with a third of the egg mixture. Repeat until all the potatoes and egg mixture have been used up. Sprinkle with the grated cheese.

Bake for 40 minutes, or until the potatoes are tender and the top of the dish is golden.

## Tip

For a different taste, use half potatoes and half carrots, or add some streaky bacon to the potato layers.

# Chicken and potato soup

*Serves 6*

This dish is a great winter warmer and, above all, requires very little hands-on time. Just put the ingredients together in a deep saucepan and wait until it's all cooked and ready to enjoy. Combining starch and proteins, this soup is both filling and healthy.

2 cloves garlic

2 onions

5 potatoes

1 leek

400g boneless and skinless chicken breasts

3 tablespoons chicken stock powder

750ml water, tepid

salt and pepper

2 tablespoons fresh cream (optional)

1 tablespoon freshly chopped parsley

Peel the garlic, onions and potatoes. Chop the garlic and finely slice the onions. Cut the potatoes into bite-size chunks. Clean the leek and finely slice the white and pale green parts.

Cut the chicken breasts into small pieces and place in a deep saucepan or wok. Add the prepared vegetables and the chicken stock powder, and add the tepid water. Season with salt and pepper. Cover and simmer for 30 to 40 minutes, stirring occasionally.

Before serving, mix in the fresh cream if used, and sprinkle with freshly chopped parsley. Serve hot.

# Potato and bacon cakes

*Serves 6*

Children will love these little cakes, which are easy to make and fun to eat. Baking them in the oven instead of deep-frying them in oil makes them healthier and just as tasty. Any leftovers can be frozen and reheated when required.

### Tip

Alternatively, these cakes may be cooked in a frying pan. Heat up a tablespoon of oil in a pan and drop in a spoonful of the potato and bacon mixture; flatten slightly to shape into a cake and repeat to fill the pan. Fry until each potato cake is golden on the underside, then turn over and fry the other side.

6 potatoes

2 carrots

2 onions

150g bacon

1 tablespoon freshly chopped parsley

3 eggs

3 tablespoons flour

70g cheese, grated

Preheat the oven to 180°C (350°F) fan bake. Grease an ovenproof tray.

Peel the potatoes, carrots and onions. Grate in a food processor. Finely chop the bacon. Mix the grated vegetables, bacon, parsley and eggs together in a bowl. Add the flour.

Place spoonfuls of this mixture onto the prepared tray and shape into flat, round cakes. Sprinkle with grated cheese. Bake for 30 minutes or until golden. Repeat until all the potato mixture has been used up. Serve with a salad and sour cream if desired, as a light meal or as a side vegetable.

# Potato and fish mash

*Serves 4*

This basic dish should be a hit with children. Mash is an all-time favourite with young ones, and this recipe suggests mixing it with fish, which children can sometimes be a little reluctant to eat. So this is a great way to get the whole family to enjoy fish without having to resort to fish fingers or fish and chips.

500g red cod

2 cloves garlic

2 bay leaves

300ml milk

300ml water

2 tablespoons dried parsley

1 lemon

100ml olive oil

700g potatoes

100ml fresh cream

30g butter

1 tablespoon fresh dill

Preheat the oven to 200°C (400°F) fan bake. Grease a deep 35 × 27cm (14 × 11 inch) rectangular oven dish.

Place the cod with the garlic, bay leaves, milk and water in a medium saucepan. Bring to a simmer. Cook for 10 minutes or until the fish is flaky. Discard the garlic and bay leaves.

Drain and flake the fish, and put in a mixing bowl with the finely chopped parsley. Add the juice of the lemon and the oil and mix well.

Cook the potatoes in the microwave. Peel and mash with a fork. Mix in the fresh cream to obtain a rough purée. Add to the fish.

Spoon this mixture into the prepared dish, scatter small pieces of butter on top, and bake for 20 minutes or until golden. Sprinkle with fresh dill and serve with a salad.

# Pumpkin

Creamy pumpkin
soup

Pumpkin
soufflés

Pumpkin and
cheese pastries

Pumpkin
tart

Pumpkin and
kumara bake

Pumpkins have a mildly sweet flavour, finely grained texture, and a bright orange colour which indicates a high content of the antioxidant beta-carotene. Traditionally, pumpkins are a Halloween and Thanksgiving staple. There are different types of pumpkin which share similar characteristics although they may have different sizes, colours, shapes and flavours. Pumpkins are a good source of vitamin A and vitamin C, potassium and fibre.

A pumpkin shell is hard to pierce. This means that while they can be stored for rather long periods of time, it can be hard to get to their tasty flesh. Once cut, pumpkin keeps for only a few days as it goes mouldy quickly. It is best to buy pumpkin whole and cut it just before use. Any extra pieces of flesh may be cut into suitable sizes for individual recipes and frozen for later use.

Pumpkins are particularly popular in soups and purées, but can be used in many other preparations. The flesh may be boiled, roasted, baked or steamed. Choose a pumpkin that is heavy for its size and free of bruises, and store it in a cool, dry place.

Pumpkin seeds, also called pepitas, are dark green in colour and are also used for culinary purposes. They have many health benefits. They have a chewy texture and a sweet, nutty flavour. They may be roasted and sprinkled on salads, breakfast cereals and other dishes.

# Pumpkin and cheese pastries

*Serves 4*

I was surprised at how sweet these pastries are. Pumpkin is naturally sweet, and this is accentuated with the addition of cream cheese and a little cumin. One thing is sure, these pastries often come out of my kitchen, to my family's delight.

8 sheets filo pastry

400g pumpkin flesh

150g cream cheese

1 egg

1 egg yolk

1 teaspoon ground cumin

freshly ground pepper

30g butter

If using frozen filo pastry, remove from the freezer and thaw in the fridge for a couple of hours. Preheat the oven to 200°C (400°F) fan bake. Grease an ovenproof tray.

Cut the pumpkin flesh into chunks, and cook in a steamer for 10 minutes. Transfer to a food processor and add the cream cheese, cut into small pieces. Process into a smooth purée. Add the whole egg and the egg yolk. Season with the ground cumin and some freshly ground pepper.

Melt the butter. Stack two sheets of filo pastry on a flat surface, lightly brush with melted butter and fold once. Place a quarter of the pumpkin mixture in the centre of the pastry and fold to obtain a triangle. Place on the prepared tray. Repeat until all the filo pastry sheets and filling have been used up.

Brush the top of each pastry with a little melted butter, and bake for 30 minutes or until golden and crispy. Serve with a side salad.

# Creamy pumpkin soup

*Serves 6*

Pumpkin soup is one of our favourite winter dinners. Every time we make it, the whole family is involved, from peeling vegetables to blending and seasoning the dish. Colourful and nutritious, this soup is perfect with a couple of slices of fresh bread spread with butter.

2 potatoes

1kg pumpkin flesh

1 teaspoon ground cumin

250ml water

40g butter

300ml milk

100ml fresh cream

salt and pepper

a few tablespoons fresh coriander

Peel and halve the potatoes. Quarter the pumpkin, deseed and spoon out its flesh. Cut it into chunks and put into a large saucepan or pressure cooker, along with the potatoes, ground cumin and water. Cook for 20 minutes.

Purée the cooked vegetables in a food processor, then return to the saucepan. Add the butter and stir until melted. Gradually add the milk and mix well. Finally mix in the fresh cream and season with salt and pepper. Mix in a little extra milk or water it you prefer a runnier consistency. Reheat, without boiling, and serve hot, sprinkled with some freshly chopped coriander.

# Pumpkin tart

*Serves 6*

I have tried many different ways to make pumpkin tarts and this one is particularly enjoyed by the whole family. I like making my own pastry, using some wholemeal flour for added nutritional value and flavour. Using yoghurt rather than cream for the filling makes it lighter, yet still very tasty.

## Savoury pastry

1 egg

125g butter, melted

125g wholemeal flour

100g white flour

## Filling

600g pumpkin flesh

30g butter

100g ham

2 eggs

150g Greek-style yoghurt

salt and pepper

Preheat the oven to 200°C (400°F) fan bake. Grease a 23cm (9 inch) round baking tin.

To make the pastry, mix the egg with the melted butter. Add the flours and mix well Press the pastry with your fingers into the base and sides of the prepared tin. Prick all over with a fork and chill for 15 minutes.

To make the filling, cut the pumpkin flesh into small chunks and place in a frying pan along with the butter. Cook for 15 minutes, tossing a few times. Transfer to a food processor and purée.

Cut the ham into pieces. Whisk the eggs lightly and mix in the pumpkin purée and pieces of ham. Add the yoghurt, and mix well. Season with salt and pepper.

Bake the pastry shell for 10 minutes. Lower the oven temperature to 180°C (350°F). Pour the pumpkin mixture into the pastry base. Bake for 25 minutes or until just set, and enjoy warm or cold.

# Pumpkin soufflés

*Serves 4*

Soufflés should be baked just before the meal and should be served as soon as they are ready. They make perfect starters, but they can also be served as a main course — in this case, serve them with a salad.

## Tip

You could alternatively use the empty pumpkin shell as a baking dish. If so, cook the whole pumpkin in boiling water for 30 minutes. Take the top off and spoon the flesh out. Set the empty shell aside and prepare the soufflé as described, simply pouring the prepared soufflé mixture into the pumpkin shell before baking.

1 pumpkin

30g butter

2 tablespoons flour

300ml milk

4 eggs, separated into yolks and whites

100g cheese, grated

3 tablespoons fresh chives

1 tablespoon cornflour

1 pinch cayenne pepper

salt and pepper

Preheat the oven to 180°C (350°F) fan bake. Grease 4 individual soufflé dishes.

Quarter the pumpkin, deseed and remove the flesh, cut the flesh into chunks, place in a steamer, and cook for 10 minutes or until tender. Purée the cooked pumpkin in a food processor.

Melt the butter in a saucepan. Remove from the heat and mix in the flour. Stir in the milk gradually, mixing until smooth. Cook over a low heat, stirring continuously for a few minutes until the sauce thickens.

Remove from the heat and mix in the egg yolks. Add the grated cheese, pumpkin purée, chopped chives, cornflour and cayenne pepper. Season with salt and pepper.

Beat the egg whites until firm, and fold delicately into the pumpkin mixture. Pour into the prepared dishes and bake for 25 minutes or until just set. Serve immediately.

# Pumpkin and kumara bake

*Serves 6*

This recipe is a good way to use up leftover pumpkin. Combined with a couple of other vegetables and herbs, and topped with a cheesy sauce, it is a quick and flavoursome dinner to make on busy mid-week days.

2 medium kumara

550g pumpkin flesh

4 cloves garlic

150ml fresh cream

150ml vegetable stock

1 tablespoon dried coriander leaves

½ pack baby spinach

salt and pepper

55g cheese, grated

Preheat the oven to 200°C (400°F) fan bake. Grease a 30 x 18cm (12 x 7 inch) ovenproof dish.

Peel and thinly slice the kumara and the pumpkin flesh. Peel and chop the garlic. Gently heat up the cream, vegetable stock and coriander.

Layer the kumara slices, pumpkin slices, garlic and baby spinach in the prepared dish. Season each layer with salt and pepper, and pour a little of the cream and stock mixture on top of each layer until all the vegetables and stock have been used up.

Cover with foil and bake for 20 minutes. Take the foil off, lower the oven temperature to 180°C (350°F), and sprinkle the top of the dish with grated cheese. Bake for another 20 minutes, then let the dish stand for 10 minutes before serving.

# Tomatoes

Tomato and
polenta bake

Tomato
tartlets

Stuffed
tomatoes

Tomato
soup

Tomato and
lentil gratin

Tomatoes are now available throughout the year; however, they are at their best and cheapest when they are in season during summer. Sweet and juicy, they are delicious raw, and are also the basis of many dishes and sauces. Although fruit in a botanical sense, they are not as sweet as other fruit and are mostly used in savoury dishes.

There are a great many tomato varieties that vary in size, shape and colour. Originating from South America, they eventually made their way to Europe, although they were originally thought to be poisonous and therefore were not very popular.

There have been many studies on the lycopene found in tomatoes, an antioxidant with many virtues, including the protection it provides against some cancers. Tomatoes are also packed with other nutrients, such as vitamin C, vitamin A and vitamin K, and they are a good source of fibre. Whether you consume them in the form of soup, sauce, raw slices or paste, increasing your intake of tomatoes is bound to have positive effects on your health.

Choose tomatoes which have a deep, rich colour and sweet fragrance, as this indicates the fruit is ripe and delicious. Tomatoes should be well-shaped, with a smooth skin and no blemishes or cracks. To keep them from ripening too quickly you can store them in the fridge, but you should take them out about 30 minutes before use for maximum flavour. Cooked tomatoes and tomato sauce freeze well.

# Stuffed tomatoes

*Serves 6*

There are as many versions of this classic dish as there are people making it. It provides a good way to use up meat leftovers (raw or cooked), while benefiting from the great nutritional value of tomatoes. Little ones are generally fond of this dish which can be fun to eat with a spoon.

6 large tomatoes

1 onion

½ bunch fresh parsley

200g beef

1 tablespoon oil

salt and pepper

2 slices wholemeal bread

1 egg

30g tasty Cheddar cheese, grated

Preheat the oven to 180°C (350°F) fan bake. Grease a deep 35 × 27cm (14 × 11 inch) large ovenproof dish.

Wash the tomatoes and cut off the side opposite the stem, setting it aside to use as a lid. Remove the seeds from the tomatoes and sprinkle the flesh with salt. Place upside down on a plate.

Peel and chop the onion. Wash and finely chop the parsley. Mince the beef, and cook over a high heat in a frying pan along with the oil, onion and parsley for about 10 minutes. Transfer to a bowl and season with salt and pepper. Remove the crust from the bread, crumble and add to the mixture. Beat in the egg and crumbed bread.

Rinse off and dry the tomatoes. Fill them generously with the beef mixture. Sprinkle with the grated Cheddar cheese and cover with the reserved lids. Place the stuffed tomatoes in the prepared dish and fan bake for 30 minutes. Serve hot.

# Tomato and polenta bake

*Serves 6*

Polenta is an Italian ingredient that is readily available from the supermarket. Traditional polenta (a kind of semolina) takes rather a long time to cook, but 'instant polenta' takes only a few minutes.

10 large tomatoes

6 cloves garlic

3 tablespoons olive oil

salt and pepper

125g mozzarella

750ml water

240g polenta

55g cheese, grated

1 teaspoon dried sweet basil

1 teaspoon dried oregano

Preheat oven to 180°C (350°F) fan bake. Grease a deep 20 x 20cm (8 x 8 inch) square ovenproof dish.

Place 6 of the tomatoes in a bowl and cover with boiling water for 30 seconds to make them easy to peel. Remove the skin, deseed, and roughly chop the flesh.

Peel and chop the garlic. Place the flesh of the tomatoes in a frying pan along with the garlic and half the olive oil. Season with salt and pepper. Cook over a medium heat for 5 minutes, tossing occasionally. Slice the mozzarella and the remaining tomatoes and set aside.

Bring the water to the boil in a saucepan. Add the polenta and mix well. Cook over a low heat, stirring for a few minutes until thick. Mix in the cooked tomatoes. Remove from the heat and mix in the grated cheese.

Spread the polenta mixture into the prepared dish and top with slices of the remianing tomatoes and mozzarella. Sprinkle with the basil and the oregano, and brush with the remaining olive oil. Bake for 25 minutes or until the tomato slices are soft and the mozzarella is melted. Remove from the oven and leave to cool before cutting into portions.

# Tomato soup

*Serves 4*

This soup makes use of canned tomatoes, which are in my opinion a pantry basic and can provide the basis of many dishes. It also means this soup can be made at any time of the year with other pantry ingredients, and provides a nice dinner when you are running short of fresh ingredients.

2 x 410g tins tomatoes in juice

1 red pepper

1 clove garlic

1 onion

2 slices wholemeal bread

4 tablespoons olive oil

2 tablespoons vinegar

250ml water

1 tablespoon dried sweet basil

1 teaspoon dried rubbed mint

1 tablespoon sugar

salt and pepper

70g feta cheese

Place the tomatoes in juice in a food processor. Wash and halve the pepper and remove the seeds. Cut into pieces and add to the tomatoes. Peel and slice the garlic and onion. Remove the crust from the bread and add the bread to the tomatoes, along with the garlic and onion. Process into a smooth purée.

Add the olive oil, vinegar and water, and mix until well combined. Mix in the sweet basil, rubbed mint and sugar, and season with salt and pepper. Transfer to a deep saucepan and bring to a simmer. Cover and cook over a low heat, stirring occasionally, for 20 minutes.

Before serving, add the crumbled feta cheese and simmer for another 10 to 15 minutes. Serve with some crusty bread.

# Tomato tartlets

*Serves 4*

These tartlets are particularly tasty and don't last for very long with hungry people around. If preferred, you can make one large tart but little tartlets are rather convivial as finger food for a buffet-style dinner.

150g shortcrust pastry

16 medium tomatoes

1 onion

2 cloves garlic

½ bunch fresh parsley

40g butter

2 bay leaves

1 teaspoon sugar

salt and pepper

2 eggs

240g cheese, grated

Preheat the oven to 200°C (400°F) fan bake. Grease 4 individual tartlet baking tins.

Divide the pastry into 4 portions and press with your fingers into the base and sides of the prepared tins. Prick all over with a fork and chill for 15 minutes.

To make the filling, place 12 of the tomatoes in a bowl and cover with boiling water for 30 seconds to make them easy to peel. Remove the skin, deseed and roughly chop the flesh. Peel and finely chop the onion and garlic. Wash and finely chop the parsley. Place all these ingredients in a frying pan with the butter and bay leaves.

Cook uncovered over a medium heat, stirring occasionally until you obtain a smooth, thick sauce. Remove the bay leaves and discard. Mix in the sugar, and season with salt and pepper.

Transfer to a bowl and add the beaten eggs to the tomato sauce. Mix in 200g of the grated cheese.

Bake the pastry shells for 5 to 10 minutes until crispy and slightly golden. Lower the oven temperature to 180°C (350°F). Fill the pastry cases with the tomato mixture. Slice the remaining tomatoes and use them to top the pastries. Sprinkle with the remaining grated cheese. Bake for 10 minutes or until the cheese has melted. Enjoy warm or cold, sprinkled with chopped parsley.

# Tomato and lentil gratin

*Serves 6*

Lentils are not commonly used, yet their nutritional value is high. A good source of iron and vitamins, they ought to be a regular part of everyone's diet. This recipe provides an interesting way to include them in a family-friendly dish.

3 onions

2 cloves garlic

1 tablespoon dried sweet basil

3 tablespoons oil

2 x 250g tins lentils in brine

320g cooked rice

5 tomatoes

1 teaspoon dried mixed herbs

40g cheese, grated

salt and pepper

Preheat the oven to 180°C (350°F) fan bake. Grease a deep oven dish.

Peel and slice the onion and garlic. Place in a frying pan along with the salt and pepper, sweet basil and half the oil. Cook over a medium heat for a few minutes.

Drain the lentils and add to the pan. Mix well and add the cooked rice. Spread over the bottom of the prepared dish.

Halve the tomatoes and place them, flat side up, on top of the lentil and rice mixture. Brush with the remaining oil, and sprinkle with the mixed herbs and grated cheese. Bake for 35 minutes and enjoy.

# Meat

Ham and olive cake

Chorizo and vegetable casserole

Meatballs in tomato sauce

Beef and carrot casserole

Sautéed pork

Red meat is an excellent source of protein, vitamin B and iron. However, its saturated fat has been linked to heart disease and some types of cancers, so limit red meat consumption to two to three times a week.

Meat is highly perishable so should always be refrigerated, or frozen if you have more than you require for a particular recipe. Thaw uncooked frozen meat in the fridge, not at room temperature, so plan ahead, as it takes up to 24 hours. Meat can also be thawed in cold water, by leaving it in its original wrapping or in a watertight bag and changing the water every 30 minutes. Marinating the meat should also be done in the fridge. It is best to discard the used marinade as it may contain bacteria; so if you need some for a sauce or dip, reserve a portion *before* adding the raw food.

Meat is versatile and is available in a wide variety of cuts, making it the main component of myriad recipes. Prices vary depending on the cut of meat, generally according to its flavour, texture, fat content and degree of tenderness. The cooking method is also determined by the cut of meat to be cooked. Tender cuts of meat benefit from fast, high-heat cooking while tougher cuts benefit from slower and longer cooking times at a lower temperature.

# Meatballs in tomato sauce

*Serves 6*

These meatballs can be made with either beef or lamb and are full of protein and iron. To increase their fibre content, I use wholemeal bread rather than white bread. This dish is great if you have small children as finger food allows them to feed themselves, which they love.

4 slices wholemeal bread, crust removed

100ml milk

2 cloves garlic

2 small shallots

300g beef or lamb steak

2 eggs

1 tablespoon freshly chopped mint

2 tablespoons flour

salt and pepper

Preheat the oven to 180°C (350°F) fan bake. Grease an ovenproof tray.

Remove the crust from the bread and crumb. Place in a bowl. Cover with the milk.

Peel the garlic and shallots. Place in a food processor with the beef. Mince, then add this mixture to the bread. Mix well. Beat in the eggs and chopped mint. Lastly, mix in the flour. Season with salt and pepper.

Place spoonfuls of this mixture onto the prepared tray, shape into small balls and bake for 20 minutes. Stick a toothpick into each meatball and serve warm with a tomato-based dip and a few lettuce leaves.

# Ham and olive cake

*Serves 6*

This simple savoury cake is delicious either on its own or with a mixed salad, and is best served warm. All there is to do is to mix the ingredients together, making it foolproof.

100g butter

3 eggs

125g flour

100g ham

70g cream cheese

15 pitted black olives

1 tablespoon fresh chives

salt and freshly ground pepper

2 tablespoons breadcrumbs

Preheat the oven to 180°C (350°F) fan bake. Grease a 23 × 12cm (9 × 5 inch) loaf tin.

Melt the butter in a saucepan. Transfer to a bowl and beat in the eggs. Beat in the flour and mix well to remove any lumps.

Cut the ham and cream cheese into small pieces and add to the mixture, along with the pitted olives. Wash and dry the chives and finely chop. Add to the mixture, season with salt and freshly ground pepper, and pour into the prepared tin.

Sprinkle with breadcrumbs and bake for 30 minutes or until golden. Transfer to a serving dish, cut into slices, and serve warm.

# Beef and carrot casserole

*Serves 6*

This dish is inspired by a traditional French dish that my mum often made for us and that I loved. Here I have come up with my own version, adapted from the ingredients and cooking methods commonly used in France.

500g beef schnitzel

1 tablespoon flour

1 tablespoon dried thyme

30g butter

salt and pepper

8 carrots

3 onions

150ml white wine

300ml water

Cut the beef into bite-size pieces and sprinkle with the flour. Place in a deep saucepan with the thyme and butter and cook over a high heat for a few minutes, tossing a few times, until cooked through. Season with salt and pepper.

Peel and finely slice the carrots and onions. Add to the beef. Pour the wine and water over the beef and vegetables and bring to a simmer. Cover and cook for 30 minutes. Adjust the seasoning and serve with some long-grain rice or steamed potatoes.

# Chorizo and vegetable casserole

*Serves 6*

This Spanish-inspired dish is both spicy and filling. I like the large quantity of sauce that can be soaked up with a few slices of fresh bread!

1 onion

200g pepperoni stick

2 tablespoons oil

5 medium potatoes

2 cloves garlic

1 teaspoon ground cumin

1 x 410g tin tomatoes in juice

½ x 410g tin peas

½ x 300g tin chickpeas

1 tablespoon vegetable stock powder

300ml water

salt and pepper

Peel and slice the onion. Slice the pepperoni stick. Heat the oil in a deep frying pan and fry the onion and pepperoni slices over a high heat for a few minutes.

Peel and quarter the potatoes. Peel and grate the garlic. Add to the frying pan with the ground cumin, and stir. Cook for a couple of minutes.

Add the tomatoes in juice, roughly chopped, as well as the drained peas and chickpeas. Dilute the vegetable stock powder in the hot water and pour over the vegetables.

Bring to the boil. Cover and simmer for 30 minutes or until the potatoes are tender. Season with salt and pepper, and serve hot.

# Sautéed pork

*Serves 6*

This dish takes little time to prepare and is wholesome and nutritious. Any leftovers can be frozen, or will keep in the fridge for a couple of days.

2 tablespoons sultanas

700g pork schnitzel

1 carrot

1 onion

½ celery stalk

3 tablespoons oil

30g butter

1 x 410g tin tomatoes in juice

salt and pepper

200ml water

Place the sultanas in a bowl and cover with some tepid water. Leave for a few minutes, then drain and set aside. Cut the pork into bite-size pieces and set aside.

Peel the carrot and onion. Chop into small pieces. Wash the celery and finely slice. Place the vegetables in a frying pan with the oil. Cook over a medium heat for a few minutes. Remove from the pan and replace with the meat and butter. Cook the meat through.

Return the vegetables to the pan. Purée the tomatoes in a food processor and add to the pan. Season with salt and pepper and cover with the water. Simmer over a low heat for 30 minutes. Lastly add the sultanas and cook for another 5 minutes. Transfer to a serving dish and serve hot with rice.

# Chicken

Chicken and mushrooms in blue cheese sauce

Baked chicken thighs

Chicken filo tart

Chicken and tomato casserole

Chicken and lemon casserole

Chickens are raised primarily for meat and eggs. One of the most popular and versatile meats available, chicken may be roasted, grilled, boiled, or stewed; served on its own, with fries, pasta or vegetables; enhanced by various aromatic herbs and spices — there is a chicken recipe for every taste.

A healthy alternative to red meat, chicken is the world's primary source of animal protein (it also contains niacin and selenium). Meat-lovers who wish to reduce their fat intake should look at consuming more chicken, in particular chicken breast, provided they discard the skin. Of course, the cooking method also has an impact on the amount of fat contained in the finished dish.

Chicken may be prepared in a multitude of ways, from southern fried chicken to tandoori chicken, Thai chicken salad, barbequed chicken skewers or chicken soup, to name just a few. If possible, look for chickens that have been organically raised rather than battery chickens, as they will have had better living conditions and will be tastier, too. Chicken freezes well and is a must to have in your freezer for impromptu dinner parties.

Always be careful when handling raw chicken, making sure it does not come into contact with other foods and using different utensils for raw meat and vegetables. To be safe and limit the risks of contamination, always wash the chopping board, utensils and your hands in hot soapy water after handling raw chicken.

# Chicken filo tart

*Serves 6*

Filo pastry is used in many Greek national dishes. I like its crispiness and the fact that, being made mostly from flour and water, it is virtually fat-free and therefore a great alternative to the traditional puff pastry and short pastry. If you buy filo pastry frozen, put it in the fridge before use until it has completely thawed. Filo pastry sheets are very fragile and will break if they are still partly frozen when handled. If using fresh filo pastry, you may want to freeze any leftover sheets; alternatively, the unused sheets can be kept for up to a week in the fridge.

1 x 210g tin mushrooms in brine

1 onion

2 tablespoons oil

300g boneless and skinless chicken breast

1 teaspoon dried mixed herbs

3 whole eggs

100g sour cream

10 sheets fresh or frozen filo pastry

1 egg yolk

55g Cheddar cheese, grated

Preheat the oven to 180°C (350°F) fan bake. Grease a 23cm (9 inch) round ovenproof dish.

Drain and slice the mushrooms. Peel and slice the onion. Put in a frying pan with 1 tablespoon oil and cook over a medium heat for 10 minutes or until tender. Set aside.

Cut the chicken into bite-size pieces. Place in the frying pan with the remaining oil and dried mixed herbs. Cook over a high heat, tossing the chicken pieces occasionally, until cooked through.

Break the whole eggs into a mixing bowl. Beat in the sour cream. Mix in the cooked chicken and mushrooms.

Line the bottom and sides of the prepared dish with the filo pastry sheets. Pour the filling on top, and use the egg yolk to lightly brush the exposed parts of the filo pastry. Sprinkle with grated Cheddar cheese. Bake for 35 minutes, or until the filling is just set and the filo pastry is crispy and golden.

# Chicken and mushrooms in blue cheese sauce

*Serves 6*

With a very short preparation time and no particular skills required, this recipe is a great solution for the days when unexpected guests turn up and you need to come up with a lovely meal in a hurry.

6 portobello mushrooms

4 cloves garlic

30g butter

2 tablespoons dried rubbed parsley

500g boneless and skinless chicken breasts

1 tablespoon oil

100ml fresh cream

80g creamy blue cheese, crumbled

salt and pepper

300g fettuccine pasta

Wipe the mushrooms clean and cut each one into 8 pieces. Peel and finely chop the garlic. Place the mushrooms and garlic in a frying pan with the butter. Sprinkle with the rubbed parsley and cook over a high heat for 10 minutes or until tender. Set aside.

Cut the chicken breast into bite-size pieces. Place in the frying pan with the oil and cook thoroughly. Mix in the fresh cream and the crumbled blue cheese. Stir over a low heat for a couple of minutes until the cheese is fully melted. Mix in the mushrooms, and season with salt and pepper. Simmer for a few more minutes, stirring occasionally.

Fill a pan with boiling water and add 1 teaspoon of salt. Cook the pasta *al dente* as per the instructions on the packet. Drain well. Serve immediately with the chicken and mushrooms in blue cheese sauce.

# Chicken and tomato casserole

*Serves 6*

Tinned tomatoes in juice are cheap, extremely useful and can provide the basis for many last-minute dishes. I have also added some white button mushrooms to the mix, as they marry well with the other flavours of this dish.

8 white button mushrooms

½ bunch fresh parsley

5 cloves garlic

30g butter

600g skinless and boneless chicken breasts

1 x 410g tin tomatoes in juice

salt and pepper

## Potato purée

6 large potatoes, boiled

30g butter

225ml milk

Wipe clean and finely slice the mushrooms. Wash, dry and chop the parsley. Peel and slice the garlic. Place the mushrooms, garlic and half the chopped parsley in a frying pan with the butter. Cook over a medium heat for 10 minutes.

Set aside and replace with the sliced chicken breasts. Cook over a high heat for 10 minutes or until cooked through, stirring occasionally.

Purée the tomatoes in a food processor. Pour over the chicken. Season with salt and pepper and simmer for 15 minutes over a low heat, stirring once or twice.

In the meantime, peel and halve the potatoes. Cook in a steamer for 10 to 15 minutes. Transfer to a mixing bowl and add the butter and milk. Process into a smooth purée with a food processor, adding more milk if necessary to obtain the desired consistency. Mix in the remaining chopped parsley, and season with salt and pepper.

To serve, divide the chicken and tomato casserole between 6 plates and accompany with a serving of potato purée.

# Baked chicken thighs

*Serves 4*

Chicken thighs are not as popular as chicken breasts; however, spiced up well and accompanied with some vegetables and melted cheese as in this recipe, they make a great inexpensive meal.

500ml water

1 teaspoon chicken stock powder

4 chicken thighs

2 peppers

8 slices Colby cheese

1 tablespoon oil

1 teaspoon Cajun spice

1 teaspoon Moroccan spice

1 tablespoon cracked pepper

Preheat the oven to 180°C (350°F) fan bake. Grease a 20 x 20cm (8 x 8 inch) ovenproof dish.

Bring the water to the boil in a large saucepan. Add the chicken stock powder and the chicken thighs. Poach for 15 minutes and remove from the saucepan. Set aside 100ml of the stock. Halve and deseed the peppers. Chop into small pieces.

Wrap each chicken thigh with a couple of slices of cheese and place in the prepared dish. Lightly brush the top with the oil and sprinkle with the Cajun spice, Moroccan spice and cracked pepper. Scatter the chopped peppers around the chicken thighs and pour the reserved stock into the dish.

Bake for 25 minutes or until the cheese is melted and golden. Serve with a green salad.

# Chicken and lemon casserole

*Serves 6*

This dish is inspired by Moroccan cuisine and has a refreshing, tangy flavour. The combination of spices and herbs is crucial to giving this dish its flavour and intensity. Taste and adjust if necessary to ensure the strength of the seasoning suits your personal taste.

4 skinless and boneless chicken breasts

2 chicken thighs

3 tablespoons oil

1 teaspoon ground cumin

1 teaspoon ground ginger

500ml water

1 tablespoon vegetable stock powder

2 lemons

2 tablespoons fresh coriander

1 onion

2 cloves garlic

100g pitted black olives

salt and pepper

500g couscous

30g butter

Place the chicken breasts and thighs in a deep saucepan with the oil. Add the ground cumin and ground ginger. Cook over a medium heat on all sides until golden and cooked through. Heat up the water and add to the saucepan along with the vegetable stock powder.

Wash and slice the lemons. Wash and chop the coriander. Peel and slice the onion and garlic. Add to the saucepan, along with the olives. Season with salt and pepper, and simmer over a low heat for 20 minutes.

Pour the couscous in a bowl and cover with boiling water to reach 1cm (½ inch) over the couscous. Cover and leave for a few minutes until the water has been absorbed. Using a fork, separate the couscous grains. Mix in diced butter until melted. Cook in a microwave oven for a couple of minutes, and serve with the chicken and lemon casserole.

# Mince

Stuffed
vegetables

Chili con
carne

Cottage
pie

Mince and
walnut pastries

Lasagna

Often regarded as a humble meat, mince is versatile as well as economical. Lamb, chicken or pork offer nice alternatives to traditional minced beef. Minced meat is generally quite a bit cheaper than regular cuts of meat, but price varies according to leanness. To get good-quality mince, be prepared to pay a little extra.

Personally, I like to look at what meats are on special, so I can buy tasty, good-quality meat at a reasonable cost which I can then mince myself. Mincing in a food processor takes very little effort, and it allows any excess fat to be removed. Mince has a relatively higher risk of contamination and causing food poisoning, so mincing meat at home means that I can do so when I need it and use it right away. Minced meat should always be cooked right through to avoid any risk of food poisoning. Leftovers should be refrigerated, thoroughly reheated and eaten quickly.

Mince can be used in many different preparations, from traditional lasagna and cottage pie to more imaginative gourmet dishes. Patties, pies, meat loaves, stuffed vegetables, and pasta sauces are just a few examples of how you can make good use of this ingredient. Leftover roast meat can be minced and used in any of these dishes. Another advantage of mince is that it is easier for children to chew, and so is a good way to introduce meat into their diet.

# Cottage pie

*Serves 6*

This dish is known in France as *Hachis Parmentier* and I remember it fondly as one of my favourite childhood dishes. Traditionally made with beef, you could use any other meat leftovers to make this dish.

1 onion

300g beef

2 tablespoons oil

salt and pepper

1 tablespoon fresh cream

12 potatoes

55g butter, diced

200ml milk

Preheat the oven to 180°C (350°F) fan bake. Grease a deep 35 × 27cm (14 × 11 inch) rectangular oven dish.

Peel and finely chop the onion. Mince the beef in a food processor. Cook over a high heat in a frying pan along with the oil and chopped onion. Season with salt and pepper. Remove from the heat and mix in the cream.

Peel the potatoes and cook in a steamer for 15 minutes. Transfer to the food processor and add the diced butter. Gradually mix in the milk while processing into a purée. Season with salt and pepper and mix well.

Spread the mince at the bottom of the prepared dish and top with the potato purée. Bake for 35 minutes or until the top of the dish is golden and crispy. Serve hot with a green salad on the side.

# Stuffed vegetables

*Serves 6*

Mince can be used in many types of stuffing, and goes well with vegetables. I have used minced chicken with peppers and courgettes in this recipe, but, depending on what's in season, other vegetables may be used.

3 courgettes

3 peppers

2 slices wholemeal bread

55ml milk, tepid

200g leftover cooked chicken

1 onion

3 cloves garlic

2 tablespoons oil

1 teaspoon dried mixed herbs

1 teaspoon dried rubbed parsley

1 x 410g tin tomatoes in juice

salt and pepper

150g cooked brown rice

3 tablespoons breadcrumbs

Preheat the oven to 180°C (350°F) fan bake. Grease 2 deep 35 × 27cm (14 × 11 inch) rectangular oven dishes.

Wash and dry the courgettes and peppers. Halve the courgettes and remove the stalk. Spoon their flesh out and set aside. Halve and deseed the peppers. Remove the crust of the bread and put the bread in a bowl. Pour the tepid milk on top. Mince the chicken.

Peel and mince the onion and garlic. Place in a frying pan with the oil, mixed herbs and rubbed parsley. Cook for 5 minutes, stirring a few times.

Purée the tomatoes and the flesh of the courgettes in a food processor. Add to the pan along with the chicken. Season with salt and pepper and simmer for 15 minutes over low heat.

Transfer to a bowl and add in the bread and the brown rice. Mix well. Place the courgette and pepper halves at the bottom of the prepared dishes. Fill with the mince mixture and sprinkle with breadcrumbs. Bake for 45 minutes and serve hot.

# Mince and walnut pastries

*Makes 8*

These pastries are an original way to serve mince. They may be served as finger food at a buffet party, or with a green salad as a main meal. They feature on my children's list of 'things to do again' (a rather long list, I must say).

300g puff pastry (2 sheets)

1 egg yolk

1 tablespoon milk

## Filling

1 shallot

300g cooked lamb

70g walnut halves

2 tablespoons fresh cream

3 tablespoons fresh basil

2 eggs

salt and pepper

Preheat the oven to 180°C (350°F) fan bake. Grease an ovenproof tray.

Peel and finely chop the shallot. Mince the lamb in a food processor. Chop the walnuts. Mix the shallot with the lamb and add the chopped walnuts, fresh cream, chopped basil and eggs. Season with salt and pepper and mix until well combined.

Spread out the pastry and cut into 8 squares. Spread a little of the mince and walnut mixture in the middle of a square and roll. Press both ends together to seal the rolls. Repeat until all the pastry and filling have been used up and place on the prepared tray.

Mix the egg yolk with the milk and use to brush the top of each pastry. Bake for 12 to 15 minutes, or until crispy and golden. Serve hot with a mixed salad on the side.

# Chili con carne

*Serves 6*

This famous Mexican speciality has featured on the menus of Western restaurants for many years. Thanks to tinned tomatoes and tinned red kidney beans, this dish is very quick to prepare and makes a wonderful mid-week dinner.

2 onions

2 cloves garlic

400g beef

30g butter

1 × 410g tin tomatoes in juice

1 × 400g tin red kidney beans

1 teaspoon chili powder (adjust amount according to level of spiciness desired)

1 teaspoon ground cumin

1 teaspoon dried oregano

salt and pepper

1 tablespoon fresh parsley

Peel the onions and garlic. Mince in a food processor together with the roughly chopped beef. Place in a deep frying pan with the butter. Cook over a high heat, stirring, until the meat is cooked through.

Add the roughly chopped tomatoes in juice. Drain the red kidney beans and add to the pan. Mix in the chili powder, ground cumin and oregano. Season with salt and pepper. Cover and simmer over a low heat for 30 minutes, stirring occasionally, to let the flavours develop. Sprinkle with some freshly chopped parsley and serve with long-grain rice.

# Lasagna

*Serves 6*

A classic dish if ever there was one — every family has their own favourite lasagna recipe. Here is my basic recipe; very uncomplicated, but very tasty.

400g beef (eg, rump steak or other cut of beef)

1 onion

2 carrots

½ bunch fresh parsley

30g butter

1 teaspoon dried mixed herbs

2 x 410g tins tomatoes in juice

salt and pepper

1 x 200g pack lasagna

100g Cheddar cheese

Preheat the oven to 180°C (350°F) fan bake. Grease a deep 35 × 27cm (14 × 11 inch) rectangular oven dish.

Mince the beef in a food processor. Peel and finely chop the onion. Peel and grate the carrots. Wash and finely chop the parsley. Place all these ingredients in a frying pan with the butter and dried mixed herbs. Cook over a high heat, stirring well, until the meat is cooked through.

Mash the tinned tomatoes in a bowl and add half of them to the pan. Season with salt and pepper. Cover and simmer over a low heat for 15 minutes.

Place a layer of lasagna sheets at the bottom of the prepared dish and cover with half the mince mixture. Repeat. Top the dish with a layer of lasagna sheets and cover with the remaining tomatoes. Sprinkle with grated Cheddar cheese and bake for 40 minutes. Enjoy with a side salad.

# Eggs

Scrambled eggs
pastries

Egg and
spinach gratin

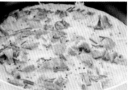

Smoked salmon
flan

Egg and
potato salad

Kumara
omelette

Eggs are available year-round and are one of the most versatile ingredients used in cooking, both in sweet and savoury dishes. They are widely used as a binding agent in sauces as well as in baking, but are also delicious on their own. They can be hard-boiled, soft-boiled, fried, scrambled, poached, pickled or even eaten raw.

The unique chemistry of eggs makes them useful in various preparations.The yolk and the white are often used separately for different purposes. Egg yolks act as an emulsifier, while egg whites are great to make aerated dishes.

A good source of low-cost, high-quality protein, eggs also provide choline, a nutrient needed for good health and brain function.

Eggs are often labelled according to their size and to the hen's diet and living conditions (eg, battery eggs, barn eggs, free-range eggs). They are best refrigerated and will keep fresh for up to a month. Eggs are one of the foods most commonly associated with allergic reactions, but health safety concerns about eggs centre on the salmonella bacteria they may contain. Salmonella is only destroyed when food is cooked at a high temperature. For this reason, raw or soft-cooked eggs carry a small risk of food poisoning and should be avoided by vulnerable people (eg, pregnant women and the elderly).

# Smoked salmon flan

*Serves 6*

Smoked salmon is not a cheap ingredient, but thanks to its strong flavour only a small amount needs to be used to add great taste and a feeling of luxury. The combination of eggs, vegetables and milk makes this a complete dish providing carbohydrates, proteins and calcium among other things. Depending on the season and the content of your fridge, you may vary the vegetables used. In the middle of winter, carrots, leek or broccoli would make a good substitute for the courgettes.

| | |
|---|---|
| 4 potatoes | salt and pepper |
| 2 courgettes | 55g smoked salmon |
| 6 large eggs | 30g Cheddar cheese |
| 250ml milk | 1 teaspoon dried dill |

## Tip

For advice on how to cook egg-based recipes using the *bain-marie* method, refer to the tip on page 12.

Preheat the oven to 160°C (325°F) fan bake. Grease a 23 × 12cm (9 × 5 inch) loaf tin.

Peel the potatoes. Clean the courgettes and cut off the stalks. Finely slice the potatoes and courgettes. Line the bottom of the prepared tin with the potato slices.

Beat the eggs with the milk in a mixing bowl. Season lightly with salt and pepper. Pour half of this mixture over the potatoes. Top with small pieces of smoked salmon and slices of courgettes. Cover with the remaining egg mixture.

Grate the Cheddar cheese. Sprinkle the top of the dish with the dill and grated cheese. Half-fill a large rectangular dish with water. Place the smaller dish containing the smoked salmon and courgette flan inside this dish. Bake for 40 minutes or until just set.

Remove from the oven and leave to cool for an hour. Take the flan out of the tin and place on a serving dish. Cut into slices and serve warm or cold, as a starter or as a light main.

# Scrambled eggs pastries

*Serves 4*

Simple and quick to make, these pastries are sure to add appeal to your brunch menu. Only make the quantity required, as they should be eaten as soon as they are ready and will not keep well.

30g butter

2 tablespoons fresh chives

1 tablespoon dried sweet basil

1 teaspoon dried oregano

salt and pepper

2 tablespoons sour cream

2 sheets puff pastry

1 egg yolk

1 tablespoon milk

8 eggs

Preheat the oven to 200°C (400°F) fan bake. Grease an ovenproof tray.

Heat up the butter in a frying pan. Add the freshly chopped chives, sweet basil and oregano. Cook over a high heat for a couple of minutes, stirring. Season with salt and pepper. Mix in the sour cream. Remove from the heat and set aside.

Cut each pastry sheet into 4 squares. Place 4 pastry squares onto the prepared tray and top each one with another pastry square. Press the sides together and cut off a smaller square in the centre of the top pastry square.

Mix the egg yolk with the milk. Lightly brush the pastry with the egg yolk, and bake for 10 minutes or until the top pastry squares are puffed and golden. Lower the oven temperature to 150°C (300°F) and bake for another 10 minutes.

Break the eggs in a bowl set over a saucepan filled with gently simmering water. Whisk with a fork and mix in the cooked herbs. Whisk until just set. Divide the scrambled eggs between the puff pastry cases and serve immediately, with a green salad on the side.

# Egg and potato salad

*Serves 6*

A recipe can hardly get any simpler than this one. This salad will be a hit as a refreshing summer lunch, and it can easily be prepared by the youngest members of the family.

8 eggs

6 potatoes

1 lettuce heart

4 tablespoons mayonnaise

salt and freshly ground pepper

Place the eggs in a saucepan filled with water and cook for 10 minutes once the water starts boiling. Remove the eggs from the water and leave to cool.

Wash the potatoes and cook in a steamer for 15 minutes. Peel and cut into small chunks. Wash, dry and chop the lettuce. Peel the eggs and cut into pieces. Mix the eggs, lettuce and potatoes together in a serving bowl. Add the mayonnaise and season with salt and freshly ground pepper. Chill for at least an hour and serve.

# Egg and spinach gratin

*Serves 4*

Spinach goes particularly well with eggs, so it is worth taking advantage of the time of the year when it is in season to make this dish. The spinach mixture may be prepared ahead of time, while the fried eggs should be cooked just before serving.

1 clove garlic

2 bunches spinach

15g butter

salt and pepper

2 tablespoons sour cream

4 tablespoons cheese, grated

1 tablespoon oil

4 eggs

Preheat the oven to 180°C (350°F) fan bake. Grease 4 individual ovenproof dishes.

Peel and chop the garlic. Wash the spinach, and place in a frying pan with the butter and garlic. Cover and cook over a low heat for 10 minutes. Season with salt and pepper. Mix in the sour cream.

Divide into 4 portions and place at the bottom of the prepared dishes. Sprinkle with the grated cheese. Bake for 10 minutes or until the cheese has melted.

Heat up the oil in a frying pan and fry the eggs. Place one fried egg on top of each spinach dish and serve immediately with some buttered toast.

# Kumara omelette

*Serves 4*

An omelette is probably one of the easiest and most popular egg dishes around. I like the sweetness of the kumara, and the fresh chives are a must to enhance the flavour of any omelette.

2 kumara

12 eggs

150ml milk

salt and pepper

2 tablespoons fresh chives, chopped

1 x 410g tin green beans

4 cloves garlic

2 tablespoons oil

Peel the kumara and cook in the microwave oven on full power for 10 minutes. Insert a fine skewer in the centre to check if they are cooked, and adjust cooking time accordingly. (It will depend on your microwave's maximum power.) Set aside.

Using a fork, whisk the eggs with the milk in a mixing bowl. Season with salt and pepper. Add the freshly chopped chives and mix well.

Cut the kumara into bite-size chunks. Drain the green beans. Peel and chop the garlic. Place in a frying pan with the oil, and cook over a high heat for a few minutes, tossing a few times. Pour the egg mixture on top, and cook for a little longer until the omelette is just set. Cut into 4 portions and serve immediately.

# Fish

Smoked
fish pasta

Portuguese-style
fish fillets

Baked
red cod

Fish
risotto

Salmon filo
pockets

Available year-round, fish is a wonderful substitute for meat protein. Its versatility and the large variety on offer make it easily adaptable to all methods of cooking, whether in soups, salads, stews or baked dishes.

White-fleshed fish, such as cod, is low in fat but high in important nutrients, so is ideal for your family's diet. The nutritional benefits of fish can depend on the cooking method, though — grilled fish with veggies trounce greasy fish and chips! Salmon, with its distinctive pink-coloured flesh,

is loaded with omega-3 essential fatty acids, which are associated with mood improvement, and protection against cancer and heart disease.

As well as consumed fresh (either cooked or raw), fish may be salted, smoked or dried. Originally used as preservation techniques for easy transportation and storage, these ways of preparing fish remain popular today. As with any seafood, be sure to buy fish fresh. Fresh whole fish should be displayed buried in ice, while fish

fillets should be placed on top of ice.

Remove any bones when serving fish to children, as they are the most common food to obstruct the airway and cause choking. Some fish — in particular tuna, but also salmon, sardines and mackerel — is available canned. A tin or two in your pantry means you'll have something to take along on a picnic or to use when you run out of fresh fish.

# Baked red cod

*Serves 6*

Baking is an easy way to cook fish — all you have to do is make sure you bake it long enough to cook it, but still keep it moist! Timing will depend on the size of the fillets, so make sure you check the dish from time to time while it is in the oven.

4 slices shoulder bacon

4 red cod fillets

1 x 410g tin tomatoes in juice

3 tablespoons olive oil

100ml water

2 tablespoons dried sweet basil

2 onions

4 cloves garlic

salt and pepper

Preheat the oven to 200°C (400°F) fan bake. Grease 4 individual ovenproof dishes.

Wrap a slice of bacon around each red cod fillet. Place one wrapped fish fillet at the bottom of each dish.

Blend the tomatoes and juice in a bowl. Mix in the olive oil, water and the sweet basil. Peel and slice the onions. Peel and grate the garlic. Add to the tomatoes and mix well. Season with salt and pepper, and divide among the 4 dishes.

Bake for 20 minutes or until the fish is just cooked. Serve hot with some long-grain rice or steamed potatoes.

# Smoked fish pasta

*Serves 6*

I used to make this recipe when we went camping because using dehydrated vegetables, canned fish and tomato sauce makes it such a convenient dish. You can vary the kind of tomato sauce you use, depending on your taste and what you have on hand.

1 x 100g packet dehydrated vegetables

375g dried large shell pasta

2 tablespoons oil

1 x 450g tin chunky smoked fish fillets

1 x 750g tin tomato sauce of your choice

100g cheese, grated

salt and pepper

Place the dehydrated vegetables in a saucepan half-filled with water and bring to the boil. Simmer for 10 minutes and drain.

Cook the pasta *al dente* in a large saucepan filled with salted boiling water according to the packet instructions. Drain and transfer to a large wok along with the vegetables. Mix in the oil.

Drain and crumble the smoked fish fillets, discarding any bones. Add to the pasta, along with the tomato sauce. Mix well. Sprinkle with the grated cheese and season with salt and pepper. Cook over a medium heat, stirring occasionally until the dish is piping hot and the cheese has melted. Serve immediately.

# Fish risotto

*Serves 4*

Risotto is one of my favourite dishes, and although it takes a while to cook the result is always worth it.
Bear in mind that it will not be as moist if reheated, so make it fresh in the quantity required.

## Tip

To ensure it retains its creaminess, do not rinse risotto rice before cooking.

1 leek

2 carrots

½ teaspoon dried dill

30g butter

240g Arborio rice or other short-grain risotto rice

1l fish stock

200g fish fillets

juice of 1 lemon

2 tablespoons oil

salt and freshly ground pepper

2 tablespoons sour cream

Clean the leek and finely slice the white and pale green parts. Peel and grate the carrots. Place the leek, grated carrot, dill and butter in a deep saucepan and cook over a medium heat for 5 minutes, stirring occasionally.

Mix in the rice and stir well. Pour in the fish stock and cook, stirring continuously, until the liquid has been fully absorbed.

Cook the fish fillets in a frying pan with the lemon juice and oil. Crumble the fish and discard any bones. Delicately fold into the rice. Season with salt and freshly ground pepper. Mix in the sour cream. Leave to sit for a few minutes before serving.

# Portuguese-style fish fillets

*Serves 6*

The combination of fish with pepperoni works well; and in this recipe, as in many others, a tin of tomatoes in juice provides the basis for the sauce. Simply add a couple of seasonal vegetables for a winning dish.

150g pepperoni stick

1 onion

3 cloves garlic

2 tablespoons olive oil

1 tablespoon dried rubbed parsley

1 red pepper

1 small aubergine

1 x 410g tin tomatoes in juice

1 teaspoon dried thyme

salt and pepper

800g white fish fillets, such as hoki or
    gurnard

Slice the pepperoni stick. Peel and slice the onion. Peel and chop the garlic. Place in a frying pan with the olive oil and parsley. Cook over a high heat, stirring, for a few minutes.

Halve, deseed and chop the pepper. Dice the aubergine. Blend the tomatoes in a bowl and mix in the thyme. Add these vegetables to the pan. Season with salt and pepper.

Cover and simmer over a low heat for 15 minutes. Add the fish fillets and simmer for another 15 minutes or until the fish is just cooked. Serve immediately with some basmati rice.

# Salmon filo pockets

*Serves 6*

These filo pockets can be made with the fish of your choice. Canned fish, such as salmon, tuna or mackerel, is ideal and always at hand in the pantry.

12 sheets filo pastry
30g butter

## Filling

6 button mushrooms
1 onion
2 tablespoons fresh parsley
1 x 210g tin salmon in brine
1 egg
juice of ½ lemon
salt and pepper

Preheat the oven to 180°C (350°F) fan bake. Grease an ovenproof tray.

Clean and chop the mushrooms. Peel and chop the onion. Finely chop the parsley.

Drain the salmon, and beat with the whole egg and the lemon juice in a bowl. Mix in the chopped mushrooms, onion and parsley. Season with salt and pepper.

Stack 2 sheets of filo pastry on a flat surface. Divide the filling into 6 portions and place 1 in the centre of the pastry. Fold into a triangle. Repeat until all the filo pastry and salmon filling have been used up.

Place the salmon pockets on the prepared tray. Melt the butter, and lightly brush it over the top of the salmon pockets. Bake for 20 minutes or until crispy and golden.

# Pasta

Seafood pasta

Creamy curried pasta

Pasta and
cheese gratin

Pasta salad

Cannelloni

Pasta comes in many different shapes and sizes, and is a simple combination of water and flour. In some cases eggs may be included. Some of the best-known types of pasta include spaghetti, macaroni, fusilli, penne, lasagna, tagliatelle, fettuccine and cannelloni.

Pasta can be fresh or dried. Dried pasta keeps for long periods while fresh pasta must be kept refrigerated and consumed within a few days. Wholewheat pasta is now also easily found in supermarkets.

Pasta is most often boiled in a large amount of salted water but may also be baked in the oven as part of a dish, provided there is enough liquid in the accompanying sauce or vegetables to cook it. It can be served in myriad ways, complemented with as many different sauces as your imagination can come up with. Pesto and bolognese sauce are very common, as are simple tomato sauces, often spiced up with garlic and olive oil. Pasta is frequently served with grated cheese, especially Parmesan cheese which is a very tasty but expensive Italian cheese.

Pasta is a good source of carbohydrates, releasing energy slowly and over a long period of time. This, and the fact that it is inexpensive, makes pasta an essential staple food.

# Pasta and cheese gratin

*Serves 6*

This pasta bake only requires everyday ingredients, but is very tasty and makes enough to feed the whole family. If you have young children who are reluctant to eat meat, you may find they are more likely to accept minced meat as it is easier to chew.

1 broccoli head

½ cauliflower

1 onion

1 tablespoon fresh thyme

2 tablespoons oil

3 x 410g tins tomatoes in juice

3 cloves garlic

400g beef rump steak

30g butter

salt and pepper

350g dried pasta of your choice

100g Cheddar cheese, grated

250ml water

Preheat the oven to 180°C (350°F) fan bake. Grease a large 35 x 27 cm (14 x 11 inch) ovenproof dish.

Cut the broccoli and cauliflower florets into bite-size pieces. Peel and finely slice the onion. Place all the vegetables, along with the thyme, in a deep non-stick saucepan with the oil. Cook over a medium heat for 10 minutes, tossing a few times.

Empty 1 of the tins of tomatoes in juice into a food processor and blend until smooth. Mix into the vegetables, cover and simmer over a low heat for 20 minutes.

Peel the garlic cloves. Remove any fat from the beef and roughly chop. Place the meat in a food processor with the garlic. Mince together and transfer to a hot frying pan with the butter. Cook over a high heat for 10 minutes or until the meat is cooked through. Season with salt and pepper.

Mix the meat in with the vegetables. Add the pasta, and transfer to a the ovenproof dish. Blend the remaining tinned tomatoes in the food processor. Add with the water to the vegetables and pasta. Part of the liquid will be absorbed by the pasta while baking.

Sprinkle with grated Cheddar cheese and bake for 40 minutes. Serve hot, with a green salad if desired.

# Seafood pasta

*Serves 6*

Salmon is a nutritious and versatile fish that makes for delicious dishes. With its high protein content, as well as significant amounts of omega-3 fatty acids and vitamin D, it is a great food to include in your diet. Bear in mind, though, that it is also high in fat, and therefore does not require the addition of any oil or butter while cooking.

2 portobello mushrooms

4 courgettes

1 tablespoon oil

300g fresh salmon steaks

1 tablespoon fresh dill

350g pasta of your choice

120ml fresh cream

salt and pepper

100g tasty Cheddar cheese

Wipe the mushrooms clean and cut each one into 8 pieces. Wash and cut the ends off the courgettes. Finely slice. Place the vegetables in a frying pan with the oil and cook over a medium heat for 10 minutes or until tender. Set aside.

Place the salmon steaks in the frying pan and cook over a high heat for a few minutes. Turn over once and sprinkle with the dill. Cook until both sides are crispy but the inside is still moist and tender.

Transfer the salmon to a plate, and mix any juice released while cooking with the vegetables. Flake the salmon, making sure to remove any skin and bones.

Fill a pan with boiling water and add a teaspoon of salt. Cook the pasta *al dente* as per the instructions on the packet. Drain well.

Place the pasta in a large pan or wok and add the fried vegetables and the flaked salmon. Mix in the fresh cream, and lightly season with salt and pepper. Grate the Cheddar cheese and sprinkle it over the pasta.

Simmer for a few minutes over a medium heat, stirring occasionally, until the cheese has melted. Divide among 6 plates and serve immediately.

# Pasta salad

*Serves 6*

This pasta salad is great to take on a picnic or to enjoy as a summer lunch. The sweet basil, tomatoes, feta cheese and olive oil give it a pleasant Mediterranean flavour, while the lemon juice adds a tangy touch to the dish.

300g farfalle pasta

3 tomatoes

½ cucumber

zest and juice of ½ lemon

3 tablespoons olive oil

3 tablespoons dried sweet basil

12 pitted black olives

80g feta cheese

salt and pepper

Cook the pasta *al dente* in a large saucepan filled with salted boiling water, according to the packet instructions. Drain and leave to cool.

Place the tomatoes in a bowl and cover with boiling water for 30 seconds to make them easy to peel. Peel, deseed and dice the tomatoes and cucumber.

Mix the zest and the juice of the lemon, the olive oil and the sweet basil in a large bowl. Chop the olives and crumble the feta cheese. Add to the mixture. Season with salt and pepper and mix well.

Add the pasta and combine with the cheese and olive mixture. Fold in the diced tomatoes and cucumber and chill for at least an hour before serving.

# Creamy curried pasta

*Serves 6*

This recipe is very simple but delicious. I remember my husband, then boyfriend, making it for me shortly after we met: I was most impressed to see a young man happily peeling onions to cook for me (my dad's culinary skills were limited to opening a can if Mum was ever away). As it turned out later, my darling husband was not really a cook, but this dish remains a family tradition!

400g macaroni

3 onions

12 button mushrooms

1 tablespoon oil

1 tablespoon curry powder

200ml evaporated milk

salt and pepper

100g Cheddar cheese, grated

Cook the pasta *al dente* in a large saucepan filled with salted boiling water, according to the packet instructions. Drain.

Peel and slice the onions. Clean and slice the mushrooms. Place in a deep frying pan with the oil. Cook over a high heat for 5 minutes, tossing occasionally. Add the curry powder and combine well.

Remove from the heat and gradually add the evaporated milk. Mix in the pasta, and season with salt and pepper. Sprinkle with grated cheese and cook over a low heat for a few more minutes until the cheese has melted. Serve hot.

# Cannelloni

*Serves 6*

Cannelloni is another favourite dish from my childhood. This versatile pasta may be filled with all kinds of vegetables, meat or even fish for a seafood recipe. Make sure there is always enough liquid in the filling and sauce to cook the cannelloni properly.

1 bunch spinach

2 cloves garlic

300g chicken (or other meat)

1 tablespoon oil

1½ × 410g tins tomatoes in juice

salt and pepper

70g tomato paste

55ml fresh cream

1 packet cannelloni

150g Cheddar cheese, grated

Preheat the oven to 180°C (350°F) fan bake. Grease a deep 35 × 27cm (14 × 11 inch) rectangular oven dish.

Wash the spinach. Peel and chop the garlic. Mince the chicken and place in a frying pan, along with the spinach, garlic and oil. Cook over a medium heat, tossing occasionally, until the meat is cooked through.

Purée the tomatoes in a food processor. Add two-thirds of the blended tomatoes to the pan, season with salt and pepper, and simmer for 10 minutes. Mix in the tomato paste and the fresh cream.

Fill the cannelloni with the chicken and tomato filling. Place in the prepared dish, together with any leftover filling. Pour the remaining blended tomatoes over the cannelloni. Sprinkle with the grated Cheddar cheese and bake for 35 minutes.

# Rice

Avocado and
walnut risotto

Chickpea and
lemon rice

Oriental
rice salad

Pineapple
fried rice

Rice
cakes

Rice is a staple in many parts of the world and is sometimes eaten at every meal. In some Asian countries, 'to eat' literally translates as 'to eat rice'. Originally eaten only in Asia, this ancient food is now an important ingredient worldwide.

The milling and polishing processes needed to convert brown (or wholegrain) rice into white rice also destroy much of the vitamins, nutrients and fibre contained in this super-food. Brown rice is the whole grain with only the inedible outer hull removed. White rice has had the bran and germ removed, along with the many nutrients and vitamins contained in these layers. To get the most nutritional value, use brown rice.

Rice is often classified as short-grain, medium-grain or long-grain. Short-grain rice has the highest starch content and is the stickiest. It is best used for risottos, rice puddings, rice cakes and other recipes requiring sticky rice. Long-grain rice grains, on the other hand, tend to remain separate when cooked.

Rice should be kept in an airtight container in a cool, dry place. Rice may be steamed, cooked by the absorption method (where only the amount of water that will be absorbed by the rice is added), or by the boiling method (where it is boiled in a much larger quantity of boiling water). The cooking method depends on the variety of rice being used and the type of dish being cooked. Instructions are generally written on the packaging.

# Oriental rice salad

*Serves 6*

This exotic oriental rice salad makes a wholesome lunch or dinner. It may be eaten warm or cold and, although it will taste best eaten fresh, any leftovers will keep for a few days.

200g wholegrain rice

4 tablespoons soy sauce

2 cloves garlic

400g pak choi

200g green beans

2 tablespoons oil

1 tablespoon fresh coriander

100ml water

1 mango

2 handfuls salted peanuts

fresh mint leaves, to garnish

Bring a large saucepan filled with salted water to the boil. Add the rice, and cook for 30 to 40 minutes or until the rice is tender. Drain and mix in a bowl with the soy sauce.

Peel and chop the garlic. Wash and chop the pak choi. Cut both ends off the beans.

Heat up the oil in a wok. Add the garlic, coriander, green beans, pak choi and stir-fry for 5 minutes. Mix in the water and cook for a further 5 minutes, stirring. Stir the rice into the vegetables.

Peel and roughly chop the mango and add to the rice. Garnish with the peanuts and fresh mint leaves. Serve warm or cold.

# Avocado and walnut risotto

*Serves 4*

Here is a vegetarian dish that combines the goodness of walnuts and avocados and the wholesomeness of rice. Short-grain rice is ideal to make risotto, as it has a sticky consistency. Risotto is best made just before serving as it can become rather dry if left and reheated so try to make only the quantity required.

1 onion

3 cloves garlic

30g butter

350g Arborio rice or other short-grain risotto rice

1½l water

1 tablespoon vegetable stock powder

30g cheese, grated

2 ripe avocados

55g walnuts, chopped

salt and pepper

Peel and finely chop the onion. Peel and crush the garlic. Heat up the butter in a large saucepan, and stir-fry the onion and garlic over a high heat for a few minutes. Add the risotto rice, and stir-fry for a couple more minutes.

In another pan, bring the water to the boil and mix in the vegetable stock powder.

Pour 200ml of the stock over the rice and cook, stirring continuously, until all the liquid has been absorbed. Gradually add more stock until it has all been used up and the rice is tender.

Just before the rice is ready, mix in the grated cheese. Peel and dice the avocados and delicately fold into the risotto along with the chopped walnuts. Season with salt and pepper to taste, stand for a few minutes, then serve without delay.

# Pineapple fried rice

*Serves 4*

Here is another example of a dish combining the sweetness of fruit with savoury flavours. Fresh coriander adds a refined touch to this colourful meal.

200g long-grain rice

1 small onion

4 cloves garlic

2 tablespoons oil

½ teaspoon ground ginger

4 tomatoes

1 x 450g tin pineapple pieces in juice

2 tablespoons light soy sauce

2 eggs

15g butter

1 tablespoon fresh coriander

Bring a large saucepan filled with salted water to the boil. Add the rice and cook according to the instructions on the pack until the rice is tender. Drain.

Peel and chop the onion and garlic. Heat up the oil in a wok. Add the onion, garlic and ground ginger. Cook for a few minutes over a high heat, stirring. Mix in the cooked rice.

Halve and deseed the tomatoes. Cut into small pieces. Drain the pineapple pieces and add to the wok along with the soy sauce and tomato pieces. Stir for a few more minutes over a medium heat.

Whisk the eggs and cook over a high heat in a frying pan with the butter. Delicately fold into the fried rice. Adjust the seasoning by adding more soy sauce if required, and sprinkle with some freshly chopped coriander. Serve immediately.

# Chickpea and lemon rice

*Serves 4*

Chickpeas are not used as often as they might be, but they add a crunchy texture to other vegetables and are a good source of iron.

175g long-grain or basmati rice

2 large onions

2 cloves garlic

2 yellow peppers

2 tablespoons oil

1 tablespoon ground cumin

1 tablespoon ground coriander

1 lemon

1 x 410g tin chickpeas

1 tablespoon vegetable stock powder

250ml water

salt and pepper

Bring a large saucepan filled with salted water to the boil. Add the rice and cook according to the instructions on the pack until the rice is tender. Drain.

Peel and finely slice the onions and garlic. Halve, deseed and slice the peppers.

Heat up the oil in a deep frying pan. Add the onions, peppers and garlic. Cover and cook over a medium heat for a few minutes. Mix in the ground cumin and coriander, and stir for a couple of minutes.

Wash and slice the lemon. Add to the pan. Mix in the cooked rice and drained chickpeas. Sprinkle with the vegetable stock powder and pour in the water. Season with salt and pepper. Cook over a medium heat, stirring occasionally, until the liquid has evaporated. Serve hot.

# Rice cakes

*Serves 6*

These little cakes are easy to eat, and great served warm with a salad and a tomato-based dip. The wild rice adds some crunch, while the stickiness of the short-grain rice holds the ingredients together.

Preheat the oven to 180°C (350°F) fan bake. Grease a 35 × 27cm (14 × 11 inch) ovenproof tray.

Cook the wild rice in a saucepan filled with boiling salted water for 40 minutes or until tender. Drain well.

Peel and slice the onion. Place in a deep saucepan with the butter and oregano. Cook over a medium heat, stirring, until soft. Peel and grate the parsnips. Add to the pan with the risotto rice, and cook for a few more minutes, stirring occasionally.

Gradually add the water and bring to a simmer, stirring continuously. Sprinkle in the vegetable stock. Leave to simmer until all the liquid has been absorbed and the rice is tender and creamy, adding a little more water if necessary.

Remove from the heat and transfer to a bowl. Mix in the grated cheese, wild rice and breadcrumbs. Add the beaten eggs and flour, and mix well. Season with salt and freshly ground pepper.

Take a couple of spoonfuls of this mixture and shape into a small round cake. Place on the prepared tray and repeat until all the rice mixture has been used up. Bake for 25 minutes or until the rice cakes are golden and crispy.

100g wild rice

1 onion

30g butter

½ teaspoon dried oregano

2 parsnips

150g Arborio rice or other short-grain risotto rice

1l water

2 tablespoons vegetable stock powder

30g cheese, grated

55g breadcrumbs

2 eggs

4 tablespoons wholemeal flour

salt and freshly ground pepper

# Kiwifruit

Kiwifruit
meringues

Kiwifruit
roulade

Kiwifruit and
citrus salad

Upside-down
kiwifruit cake

Kiwifruit
crumble cake

With their bright-green flesh speckled with tiny black seeds, kiwifruit add a tropical touch to any fruit-based dessert. In New Zealand, kiwifruit are at their best from May through to October. Kiwifruit is native to China and was originally known as the Chinese gooseberry. Its name was changed to kiwifruit, to honour New Zealand's national bird, whose brown fluffy feathers resemble the skin of this fruit.

Outside New Zealand however, it is often simply referred to as 'kiwi'.

Kiwifruit are packed with vitamin C, which is necessary for the good functioning of the immune system, and are also a good source of vitamin E, potassium, folate and fibre.

When selecting kiwifruit, gently apply some pressure — a ripe, sweet fruit should yield slightly. Don't choose soft fruit which

are overripe, or those which are shrivelled or bruised. Kiwifruit can be left to ripen at room temperature, away from heat and sunlight.

Kiwifruit can be eaten raw; peeled and then sliced, or cut in half with the flesh scooped out. Kiwifruit are also great in desserts and add beautiful colour to tarts and other cakes.

# Kiwifruit meringues

*Serves 4*

These meringues are delicate to handle and are best eaten on the day they are made, when the amount of vitamin in the kiwifruit is highest. If desired, the natural yoghurt may be replaced by some sweetened whipped cream.

4 egg whites

200g sugar

3 kiwifruit

3 tablespoons natural yoghurt

Preheat the oven to 180°C (350°F) fan bake. Grease a 35 × 27cm (14 × 11 inch) biscuit tray.

Beat the egg whites into soft peaks. Gradually mix in 175g of the sugar, while beating for a couple more minutes, until the mixture is glossy. Peel and finely chop one of the kiwifruit. Delicately fold into the meringue.

Place spoonfuls of this mixture onto the prepared tray. Bake for 10 to 15 minutes or until the tops of the kiwifruit meringues are slightly brown. Remove from the oven and leave to cool.

Mix the yoghurt with the remaining sugar. Peel and slice the remaining kiwifruit. Mix half of the kiwifruit with the yoghurt.

To assemble, place a meringue on a serving plate, flat side up. Top with some kiwifruit yoghurt and cover with another meringue. Repeat until all the kiwifruit meringues and yoghurt have been used up. Garnish with the remaining slices of kiwifruit before serving.

# Kiwifruit roulade

*Serves 6*

This delicious roulade makes a great dessert or accompaniment to a cup of tea. Make sure to peel and slice the kiwifruit used for the garnish at the last minute.

## Kiwifruit cream

5 kiwifruit

100g natural yoghurt

80g sugar

100ml fresh cream

## Sponge

4 eggs

100g sugar

70g flour

30g butter

Preheat the oven to 180°C (350°F) fan bake. Grease a 35 × 27cm (14 × 11 inch) biscuit tray.

To make the kiwifruit cream, peel 4 of the kiwifruit and place in the bowl of a food processor with the natural yoghurt and sugar. Process into a smooth purée, then transfer to a bowl. Whip the fresh cream into soft peaks and fold into the kiwifruit mixture. Chill for 30 minutes.

To make the sponge, beat the egg yolks with the sugar until creamy. Mix in the sifted flour and melted butter. Beat the egg whites into soft peaks and fold into the batter. Pour this mixture onto the prepared tray.

Bake for 10 minutes or until springy to the touch. Remove from the tray and place on a damp tea towel.

Spread half of the kiwifruit filling over the sponge, leaving 2cm (1 inch) clear on all sides. Roll up from the short end and chill.

Transfer to a serving plate and cut 1cm (½ inch) off both ends. Spread the remaining kiwifruit filling over the top of the sponge and garnish with slices of the remaining kiwifruit.

# Kiwifruit and citrus salad

*Serves 4*

This fruit salad is light and refreshing and makes an ideal dessert on a warm day or after a heavy meal. For maximum nutritional value and flavour, it is best eaten fresh — make only the quantity required and prepare it just before eating.

6 kiwifruit

1 grapefruit

3 oranges

zest and juice of 1 lemon

2 tablespoons liquid honey

Peel and slice the kiwifruit and place in a mixing bowl. Halve the grapefruit and oranges. Remove the flesh and add to the bowl, along with the juice.

Finely grate the zest of the lemon and add to the fruit. Stir in the lemon juice and the liquid honey, and mix well. Chill for 20 minutes and serve.

# Upside-down kiwifruit cake

*Serves 8*

Bake this cake in a textured tin to obtain a pretty effect when it is turned over onto a serving dish. This cake is delicious when it comes out of the oven, and will keep for a couple of days in the fridge if you have any leftovers.

8 kiwifruit

4 eggs

150g sugar

1 teaspoon vanilla essence

150g unsalted butter, melted

175g flour

2 tablespoons milk

1 teaspoon baking powder

Preheat the oven to 160°C (325°F) fan bake. Grease a 23cm (9 inch) baking tin.

Peel and cut 2 of the kiwifruit into small chunks. Prepare the batter by beating the eggs with the sugar and vanilla essence. Mix in the melted butter. Add the flour, milk and baking powder, and mix until well combined. Fold in the kiwifruit pieces.

Peel and slice the remaining kiwifruit. Place at the bottom of the prepared tin and cover with the batter. Bake for 40 minutes or until golden and springy to the touch. Turn the cake over onto a serving dish. Enjoy hot or cold with a dollop of cream or yoghurt.

# Kiwifruit crumble cake

*Serves 8*

I love crumble, and I like using a crumbly topping on tarts and cakes. It adds texture as well as a sweet buttery flavour. Kiwifruit does not keep well after being peeled and chopped, so it is best to eat this cake within a day or two.

## Base

40g sugar

55g unsalted butter, melted

1 egg

125g flour

## Filling

1 x 410g tin pear halves in syrup

4 kiwifruit

30g white sugar

## Topping

70g flour

55g brown sugar

55g rolled oats

70g unsalted butter, softened

Preheat the oven to 180°C (350°F) fan bake. Grease a 20cm (8 inch) round baking tin.

To make the base, place the sugar in a bowl and combine with the melted butter. Beat in the egg and fold in the flour to obtain a smooth ball. Chill for 15 minutes. Using your fingers or the bottom of a glass, press into the base of the prepared tin. Bake for 10 minutes.

To make the filling, drain the pears and set aside 2 tablespoons of the syrup. Peel the kiwifruit and cut into chunks along with the drained pears. Place in a saucepan with the reserved syrup. Cover and cook over a medium heat for 10 minutes. Roughly mash with a fork. Mix in the sugar and leave to cool.

To make the topping, blend the flour, brown sugar, rolled oats and softened butter in a food processor to obtain a roughly crumbled mixture.

Spoon the fruit purée over the base, and scatter the crumble on top. Bake for 20 minutes or until the topping is crunchy and golden. Once cool, transfer to a serving plate and serve with custard, cream or ice cream.

# Bananas

Banana and
coconut creams

Hot winter fruit
with ice cream

Banana and
coffee tart

Banana and
pineapple crumble

Banana and
chocolate cake

Bananas are a high-energy fruit available all year round and native to the tropical region of Southeast Asia. Their very sweet taste makes them popular with children. There are many different varieties of banana, classified as either dessert bananas (yellow and fully ripe when eaten) or green cooking bananas.

Dessert bananas generally have a sweet taste and a firm, creamy flesh. Bananas are easily damaged while transported, and so export bananas are picked green to minimize damage, and are then ripened when they reach their destination.

Bananas are a valuable source of vitamin B6, vitamin C, potassium, fibre and manganese. A puréed banana is one of the first solid foods an infant can eat. Bananas may be eaten fresh, cooked and dried, and can also be used in baking. A few popular desserts include banana fritters, flambéed bananas and banana split.

When selecting bananas, consider when you want to eat them, as those with more green coloration will take longer to ripen than yellow ones or those with brown spots. Bananas should be free of bruises and their stems and tips should be intact. Baby bananas make a great snack for children.

# Banana and coffee tart

*Serves 8*

When experimenting with this tart, I wasn't sure how well it would turn out, but I was pleasantly surprised. The homemade pastry is crunchy and the bananas and coffee make a delightful combination, resulting in a morish dessert. However, like kiwifruit, bananas do not keep well after being peeled and processed, so it is best to eat this tart within a day or two of making it.

## Pastry base

80g sugar

1 egg

125g unsalted butter, melted

275g flour

## Coffee and banana custard

3 egg yolks

1 whole egg

80g sugar

55g flour

375ml milk

1 tablespoon instant coffee

4 bananas

juice of ½ lemon

30g dark chocolate

Preheat the oven to 200°C (400°F) fan bake. Grease a 23cm (9 inch) round baking tin.

To make the pastry, mix the sugar with the egg and melted butter in a bowl. Add the flour and combine well. Roll into a ball and chill for 15 minutes. Press the pastry into the bottom and sides of the prepared tin. Prick all over with a fork and chill for another 15 minutes. Bake the pastry for 10 minutes and leave to cool.

To make the coffee and banana custard, mix the egg yolks and whole egg with the sugar in a bowl. Stir in the sifted flour. Bring the milk to the boil in a saucepan. Add the instant coffee and mix well. Pour over the egg mixture. Return to the saucepan and cook over a low heat, stirring continuously, for 10 minutes or until thick. Peel and roughly mash 3 of the bananas with a fork. Fold into the coffee custard and chill for 2 hours.

Transfer the pastry case to a serving dish, and cover with the banana and coffee custard. Before serving, peel and slice the remaining banana and sprinkle with the lemon juice. Place the banana slices over the custard. Melt the chocolate with a couple of tablespoons of water to obtain a smooth sauce, and drizzle this over the top of the tart.

# Banana and coconut creams

*Serves 4*

This dessert is made in less than 20 minutes so it is ideal for when you fancy a homemade dessert on a working day. Although only the egg yolks are used in this recipe, you could use the whites later for a quick and easy pavlova to avoid wasting them. The coconut creams may be served hot or cold, depending on your taste and the season. If served cold, wait until the last minute to cook the bananas and add them to the bowls just before serving.

## Coconut creams

6 egg yolks

125g sugar

500ml coconut milk

3 tablespoons cornflour

zest of 1 lemon

## Fried bananas

2 bananas

juice of 1 lemon

30g unsalted butter

1 tablespoon desiccated coconut

To make the coconut creams, mix the egg yolks and the sugar in a bowl until pale yellow. Mix 100ml of the coconut milk with the cornflour, making sure to remove any lumps, and combine with the egg mixture.

Mix the remaining coconut milk with the zest of the lemon. Bring to the boil in a saucepan and simmer for a few minutes. Gradually pour over the egg mixture while whisking. Return the egg and milk mixture to the saucepan and cook over a low heat, stirring continuously for approximately 10 minutes or until the cream thickens.

Divide among 4 serving bowls. Chill for at least 2 hours if you intend to serve this dessert cold. Just before serving, prepare the fried bananas. Peel and slice the bananas and drizzle with the juice of the lemon. Heat up the butter in a frying pan. Add the slices of bananas, sprinkle with desiccated coconut and quickly fry on both sides. The bananas should be hot and soft, but should not be overcooked if they are to retain their texture.

Top each bowl of coconut cream with slices of fried banana, and sprinkle with a little more desiccated coconut, if desired, before serving.

# Banana and pineapple crumble

*Serves 4*

This dessert is a variation on the traditional apple crumble, one of my favourite desserts. Quick and super-easy to make, you can't go wrong with this dessert. Serve it with a scoop of ice cream for an instant hit.

4 bananas

1 × 450g tin pineapple pieces in light syrup

30g butter

## Topping

55g flour

70g brown sugar

55g rolled oats

70g unsalted butter, softened

Preheat the oven to 180°C (325°F) fan bake. Grease 4 individual ovenproof dishes.

Peel and slice the bananas. Drain the pineapple, setting the syrup aside. Place the fruit in a frying pan with the butter. Stir-fry for a few minutes until the fruit is golden. Place at the bottom of the prepared dishes and drizzle with 4 tablespoons of the reserved pineapple syrup.

To make the topping, blend the flour, brown sugar, rolled oats and softened butter in a food processor to obtain a roughly crumbled mixture. Scatter over the fruit. Bake for 30 minutes or until golden. Serve warm, with cream or ice cream.

# Hot winter fruit with ice cream

*Serves 4*

Mixing hot and cold ingredients
is interesting and results
in a successful marriage of
sensations. This recipe can be
made all year round, and is full of
nutrients while still delivering the
desired sweetness of a dessert.

100g pitted prunes

1 lemon

2 pears

3 bananas

30g butter

30g brown sugar

600ml frozen yoghurt

Pour boiling water over the prunes, and
leave to soften for a few minutes. Drain,
chop into pieces, and set aside.

Juice the lemon. Peel and cut the pears
and bananas into slices. Drizzle with
the lemon juice. Transfer to a frying pan,
along with the chopped prunes, and cook
over a medium heat with the butter for
5 minutes, tossing occasionally. When the
fruit is soft, mix in the sugar and cook for
a few more minutes.

Divide the frozen yoghurt and the hot fruit
among 4 ice-cream parfait glasses and
serve immediately.

# Banana and chocolate cake

*Serves 8*

No one can resist a piece of this banana and chocolate cake, which is both nutritious and tasty. It is delicious for afternoon tea, and can be eaten straight out of the oven, as is customary in my family, or once it has cooled down.

4 eggs

100g white sugar

55g brown sugar

1 teaspoon vanilla essence

150g unsalted butter, melted

3 ripe bananas

240g flour

1 tablespoon baking powder

70g chocolate chips

chocolate hail, to garnish (optional)

Preheat the oven to 160°C (325°F) fan bake. Grease a 23cm (9 inch) round baking tin.

Beat the eggs, white sugar, brown sugar and vanilla essence together in a bowl. Add the melted butter and mix until well combined.

Peel and roughly mash the bananas with a fork. Blend into the egg mixture. Fold in the flour and baking powder. Add the chocolate chips and mix well.

Pour this mixture into the prepared tin. Bake for 45 minutes or until a fine skewer inserted into the centre of the cake comes out clean. Serve warm or cold, with a dollop of cream or natural yoghurt and sprinkled with chocolate hail if desired.

# Apples

Apple
tartlets

Apple
pudding

Apple and
coconut cake

Apple
strudel

Apple mousse
with berry coulis

Apple trees are among the most cultivated fruit trees around, and there are hundreds of different varieties. Apples are commonly eaten fresh, but they are also widely used in baking as well, or to make apple juice, apple sauce and other preparations.

Predictably, whole, fresh apples provide the most nutritional benefits. They contain fibre (mostly in their skin) and vitamin C.

Apples are in season from late summer to early winter, but they are so widely grown worldwide that, these days, they are available in stores all year round. The colour and taste of apples vary from one variety to another. Sweet and refreshing, with a degree of tartness, they transport well and make a popular snack to take along in a bag or on a picnic.

You should look to buy firm fruit without bruises. Your choice

of variety will depend on your taste and the cooking method you have in mind: Granny Smith apples retain their texture best and are great for use in baking; while Golden Delicious, Fuji or Braeburn apples are sweeter and are delicious raw. If you are using sliced apples to add to a green salad or to a fruit salad, and want to stop them from browning, simply drizzle with a little lemon juice.

# Apple and coconut cake

*Serves 8*

This cake is simple to make and tasty, too: a winning combination in any circumstances. It can be made all year round with your favourite variety of apples.

150g sugar

1 teaspoon vanilla essence

150g unsalted butter, melted

3 eggs

100g desiccated coconut

1 apple, peeled and grated

1 tablespoon baking powder

150g flour

2 tablespoons coconut threads

## Apple filling

200ml fresh cream, refrigerated

55g icing sugar

3 apples

30g butter

Preheat the oven to 160°C (325°F) fan bake. Grease a 23cm (9 inch) round baking tin.

To make the cake, place the sugar and the vanilla essence in a bowl and add the melted butter. Mix well. Whisk in the eggs, one at a time, beating well between each addition. Mix in the desiccated coconut and the peeled and grated apple. Add the baking powder and flour, and mix well.

Pour this mixture into the prepared tin and sprinkle with the coconut threads. Bake for 40 minutes or until a fine skewer or toothpick inserted into the centre of the cake comes out clean. Take the cake out of the tin and cut into two layers. Leave to cool.

Whip the cream with the icing sugar. Peel the apples, remove the cores and cut into small pieces. Place in a frying pan with the butter and cook for 10 to 15 minutes, until tender. Set aside. Once cool, delicately fold into the sweetened cream. To assemble, transfer the bottom layer of the cake to a serving plate and cover with the apple cream. Top with the other cake layer and serve.

# Apple tartlets

*Serves 8*

With a combination of flavours and textures, these pretty tartlets are also very tasty. They present well and make a perfect dessert to impress family and friends at your next dinner party.

## Sweet pastry

55g sugar

1 egg

125g unsalted butter, melted

275g flour

## Filling

2 apples

30g butter

3 eggs

55g sugar

55ml fresh cream

2 tablespoons sliced almonds

chocolate, for garnish (optional)

Preheat the oven to 200°C (400°F) fan bake. Grease 8 individual tartlet tins.

To make the sweet pastry, mix the sugar, egg and melted butter in a bowl. Mix in the flour, shape into a ball, and chill for 15 minutes.

Press the pastry with your fingers into the bases and sides of the prepared tins. Prick all over with a fork and bake for 10 minutes. Leave to cool. Lower the oven temperature to 160°C (325°F).

To prepare the filling, peel, core and thickly slice the apples. Place in a frying pan with the butter and cook for 10 minutes, or until tender. Divide among the pastry bases.

Mix the eggs with the sugar and fresh cream, and pour this mixture over the apple slices. Scatter the sliced almonds over the egg mixture.

Bake for 20 minutes or until the egg mixture is just set. Leave the tartlets to cool in their tins. Transfer to dessert plates and serve warm or cold, with a little melted chocolate on the side if desired.

# Apple strudel

*Serves 6*

This dessert can be made with puff pastry; however, filo pastry is lighter and I like its crispiness. The apples are spiced up with vanilla and cinnamon, and cooked so as to melt in the mouth. This dessert is delicious on its own or with a scoop of vanilla ice cream.

30g sultanas

5 apples

zest of 1 lemon

1 pinch cinnamon

55g butter

55g brown sugar

8 sheets filo pastry

Preheat the oven to 200°C (400°F) fan bake. Grease a 35 x 27cm (14 x 11 inch) biscuit tray.

Soak the sultanas in hot water for 10 minutes. Peel and core the apples. Cut into chunks. Place in a frying pan with the zest of the lemon, the cinnamon and half the butter. Cook over a medium heat for 10 minutes, or until golden and tender. Mix in the brown sugar. Drain the sultanas and mix with the apples.

Melt the remaining butter. Stack 2 sheets of filo pastry, brushing each sheet lightly with the melted butter. Fold once. Place a quarter of the apple mixture onto the pastry and roll. Place on the prepared tray.

Repeat until all the filo pastry and apple mixture have been used. Brush the top of each apple roll with melted butter. Bake for 10 minutes, or until golden, and serve warm.

# Apple pudding

*Serves 6*

This pudding is a very simple recipe which can also be made with other kinds of fruit, such as pears, plums, or apricots. Serve it at the end of a meal or for afternoon tea.

6 apples

2 tablespoons water

1 teaspoon cinnamon

zest of 1 lemon

2 teaspoons liquid honey

## Topping

140g unsalted butter, melted

4 eggs

1 teaspoon vanilla essence

140g sugar

140g flour

1 teaspoon baking powder

Preheat the oven to 150°C (300°F) fan bake. Grease a deep 20 × 20cm (8 × 8 inch) ovenproof dish.

Peel, core and quarter the apples. Place in a saucepan with 2 tablespoons of water, the cinnamon, and finely grated lemon zest. Cover and cook over a medium heat for 15 minutes, or until the fruit is soft.

Remove from the heat and process into a smooth purée in a food processor. Mix in the honey. Place the fruit at the bottom of the prepared dish.

Mix the melted butter, eggs, vanilla essence and sugar together. Sift in the flour and baking powder, and fold in gently. Pour over the fruit and bake for 35 minutes, or until springy to the touch. Serve warm.

# Apple mousse with berry coulis

*Serves 6*

I like the light and fluffy texture of this mousse. The berry coulis adds both colour and flavour, and is a nice accompaniment to the apple mousse. Like other desserts made with raw eggs, this one tastes best made fresh and eaten within a couple of days.

## Mousse

3 apples

1 lemon

55ml water

1 teaspoon vanilla essence

2 egg whites

70g sugar

## Coulis

1 x 410g tin mixed berries in syrup

juice of ½ lemon

30g icing sugar

Peel and core the apples. Cut into chunks. Place in a saucepan with the lemon juice and the water. Cover and cook over a low heat for 20 minutes or until tender. Drain and transfer to a bowl. Mash into a rough purée with a fork. Mix in the vanilla essence.

Beat the egg whites until firm and mix in the sugar. Beat until the mixture is shiny. Delicately fold into the cool apple purée and chill for 2 hours.

To make the coulis, drain the berries, setting 4 tablespoons of the syrup aside. Blend the fruit in a food processor, pass through a sieve, and collect the seedless

purée in a bowl. Add the lemon juice, the icing sugar and the reserved syrup, and mix until smooth.

Layer the apple mousse and the berry coulis into 4 glass bowls or parfait glasses until all the mousse and coulis have been used up. Serve immediately.

# Lemons

Lemon
mousse

Lemon and
berry creams

Lemon and
yoghurt cakes

Lemon and
polenta cupcakes

Lemon and
jam cupcakes

Lemons are fantastic at bringing out flavours in other foods, and add a tangy taste to any dish. They are an excellent source of vitamin C, which is vital to maintaining a strong immune system.

Lemons with thin skins tend to be the juiciest. They should be yellow in colour (a green tinge indicates they are not fully ripe, and therefore are more acidic), with no soft or hard patches, and no wrinkling. Store lemons at room temperature for long life.

Always wash and dry the lemon first, to remove any pesticide residues on its skin. The juice and zest of lemons are commonly used in baking. To remove the zest, use a paring knife, cheese grater or vegetable peeler. Avoid the white pith underneath the skin, as it is bitter and should not be eaten. It is easier to extract juice from lemons at room temperature.

Lemon juice mixed with honey and boiling water makes a popular drink to help clear a cold or relieve a sore throat. Or combine lemon juice with cane sugar and sparkling water for delicious homemade lemonade!

Lemon wedges are traditionally served with fish and can be used as a garnish for drinks. Lemon juice is often used in salad dressings, and may also be used to marinate meat (to tenderize it) or fish (to neutralize the odour). Lemon juice sprinkled on apples, bananas and avocados stops them from turning brown when sliced.

# Lemon and yoghurt cakes

*Serves 8*

These little cakes resemble pancakes and have a texture similar to a baked cheesecake.
The apricot jam could be replaced with orange marmalade if desired.

4 eggs

100g sugar

2 tablespoons cornflour

400g thick natural yoghurt

100g sour cream

3 lemons

1 teaspoon vanilla essence

100g apricot jam

Preheat the oven to 200°C (400°F) fan bake. Grease 8 individual tartlet tins (I used a silicon baking tin with 4 1cm-deep impressions).

Beat the egg yolks with the sugar in a bowl until pale yellow. Mix in the cornflour, yoghurt, sour cream, and the zest of 2 of the lemons. Add the juice of 1 lemon and the vanilla essence.

Beat the egg whites until firm, and delicately fold into the mixture. Using half the mixture, divide among the prepared tins and bake for 30 minutes. Remove from the tins, and repeat to use up the mixture.

Arrange half the cakes on a serving plate. Warm up the apricot jam and dilute with a couple of tablespoons of water. Spread a little of this jam mixture on the top of each cake. Place a second cake on top of each, until all have been used up. Transfer onto 8 serving plates. Slice the remaining lemon and add a slice to each plate.

# Lemon mousse

*Serves 4*

There are many different ways to make lemon mousse, and this is one of my favourites. Lemon mousse is always delicious accompanied with a couple of thin almond or coconut biscuits.

---
**Tip**
---

Whipping cream takes little time and is simple to do, but the cream must be very cold. It may be a good idea to refrigerate the food processor bowl in which you'll be whipping the cream beforehand.

---

3 eggs, separated

150g sugar

1 tablespoon cornflour

500ml milk

2 lemons

250ml fresh cream

chopped nuts, for garnish (optional)

berry sauce, for garnish (optional)

Beat the egg yolks with 100g of the sugar in a bowl until pale yellow. Mix in the cornflour.

Place the milk in a saucepan. Grate the zest of the lemons and add to the milk. Bring to the boil, and gradually pour over the egg mixture. Return to the saucepan and cook over a low heat, stirring continuously, for 10 minutes or until thick. Mix in the juice of 1 lemon and leave to cool.

Whip the fresh cream into soft peaks. Add to the cool lemon cream. Beat the egg whites until firm and mix in the remaining sugar. Delicately fold into the lemon cream. Divide among 4 individual dessert bowls. Chill for 4 hours. Garnish with chopped nuts and berry sauce before serving, if desired.

# Lemon and polenta cupcakes

*Serves 6*

I use instant polenta to make these little cakes. Be aware, though, that polenta's fine grainy texture, as well as the ground almonds, make the cakes crumbly, so wait until they are completely cool before removing them from their tins.

240g butter

200g sugar

2 eggs

200g ground almonds

150g polenta

1 teaspoon baking powder

2 large lemons

Preheat the oven to 180°C (350°F) fan bake. Grease a mini-muffin tin.

Cream the butter and the sugar until light and fluffy. Gradually beat in the eggs.

Fold the ground almonds into the mixture. Add the polenta and the baking powder, and mix well. Mix in the zest of the lemons and 2 tablespoons of lemon juice.

Spoon this mixture into the prepared tin. Bake for about 35 minutes or until the top is golden brown. Remove from the oven and leave to cool. Once cool, remove the cupcakes from the tin and enjoy.

# Lemon and berry creams

*Serves 4*

I like being able to satisfy my cravings for berries all year round, and canned berries make a good substitute for fresh during the colder months. Of course, in summer fresh berries may be used to make this recipe.

---
## Tip

Try not to sprinkle the toasted almonds over the dessert before refrigerating or too long before serving, as they will soon become soggy.

---

450g plain Greek-style yoghurt

80g icing sugar

1 teaspoon vanilla bean paste

2 egg yolks

juice and zest of 2 lemons

100ml fresh cream

4 plain biscuits (plain shortbread or vanilla wine biscuits)

1 x 410g tin berries in syrup

30g sliced almonds

Beat the yoghurt and icing sugar in a bowl. Mix in the vanilla bean paste and the egg yolks. Add the finely grated zest of the lemons. Whip the fresh cream into soft peaks, and fold delicately into the yoghurt mixture.

Crush the biscuits and divide among 4 individual dessert bowls. Drain the berries, setting 2 tablespoons of the syrup aside. Mix the reserved syrup with the juice of the lemons and spoon over the biscuits. Top with the berries.

Pour the yoghurt mixture over the berries and chill for an hour. Toast the sliced almonds in a non-stick pan and scatter over the desserts just before serving.

# Lemon and jam cupcakes

*Serves 6*

These cupcakes appeal to children of all ages and are great for afternoon tea.

80g unsalted butter, melted

150g sweetened condensed milk

zest of 2 lemons

1 teaspoon vanilla essence

3 eggs

80g cornflour

1 teaspoon baking powder

80g desiccated coconut

6 teaspoons of your favourite jam

icing sugar, to sprinkle

Preheat the oven to 180°C (350°F) fan bake. Grease a mini-muffin tin.

Beat the melted butter with the sweetened condensed milk in a bowl. Mix in the finely grated zest of the lemons and the vanilla essence. Add the beaten eggs and mix well. Beat in the cornflour, baking powder and desiccated coconut until well combined.

Pour this mixture into the prepared tin, filling each hole only half-full as the cupcakes will rise during baking. Bake for 25 minutes or until golden. Remove the cupcakes from the tin.

Cut the top off each cupcake, and place half a teaspoon of jam in the centre. Place the top of each cupcake back on, and sprinkle with icing sugar before serving.

# Dried Fruit

Prune and
yoghurt pudding

Dried apricot and
polenta triangles

Sultana
loaf

Caramelized sultana
rice pudding

Dried fruit
filo stacks

Dried fruit is full of goodness and makes a healthy and nutritious food choice. Popular among children and sportspeople, it offers an immediate energy boost.

As well as containing minerals such as iron, manganese and potassium, dried fruit is a source of fibre and natural sugar, meaning less refined sugar needs to be added to recipes in which it features.

Dried fruit is a convenient, high-energy food often used for snacks. Raisins and sultanas are among the most popular dried fruits, but others such as dried apricots, prunes, figs and dates are also nutritionally useful as well as delicious. All are available throughout the year.

Cooked in a little butter and honey, dried fruits quickly regain their tenderness. They can be eaten on their own or served with yoghurt or ice cream. Dried fruit makes a popular addition to any plain cake and can be combined with savoury flavours for a sweet and fruity contrast.

Dried fruit can generally be stored for a long time in its original packaging; however, once opened is best kept in an airtight container and refrigerated for quick use.

# Sultana loaf

*Serves 6*

This cake is rather basic, but makes a great afternoon tea treat. Quick to make, it doesn't require any particular cooking skills and can be made by children on their own or under supervision.

55g sultanas

175g unsalted butter

175g sugar

3 eggs, separated

175g flour

1 tablespoon baking powder

Preheat the oven to 160°C (325°F) fan bake. Grease a 23 × 12cm (9 × 5 inch) loaf tin.

Soak the sultanas in hot water for 10 minutes. Drain and set aside.

Melt the butter and mix in the sugar. Beat in the egg yolks one at a time, mixing well between each addition. Mix in the sultanas. Sift in the flour and the baking powder. Beat the egg whites until firm, and fold delicately into the mixture.

Pour this batter into the prepared tin, and bake for 35 minutes or until a fine skewer or toothpick inserted into the centre of the cake comes out clean. Remove from the tin and serve warm or cold.

# Prune and yoghurt pudding

*Serves 6*

Prunes are full of nutrients and are also very sweet and moist. In this recipe, they go perfectly with the sponge fingers and the creamy yoghurt mixture. Serve cold.

10 sponge fingers

zest and juice of 1 lemon

150g pitted prunes

500g Greek-style yoghurt

100g sour cream

80g sugar

milk chocolate, grated, to garnish
  (optional)

Divide the sponge fingers among 6 dessert bowls. Finely grate the zest of the lemon and set aside. Sprinkle the sponge fingers with the lemon juice.

Pour some boiling water over the prunes and soak for 10 minutes. Drain and chop the prunes into small pieces. Scatter over the sponge fingers.

Mix the yoghurt with the sour cream and the reserved lemon zest. Beat in the sugar and mix well. Divide this mixture among the dessert bowls and refrigerate for at least an hour. Sprinkle with some grated milk chocolate before serving, if desired.

# Caramelized sultana rice pudding

*Serves 6*

Rice pudding takes a little while to prepare, as the short-grain rice it is made with takes a while to cook. As the mixture of rice and milk is prone to burning if left unattended, it should be cooked over a low heat, and stirred regularly. Enjoy this dessert warm.

175g sugar

80g sultanas

240g short-grain rice

1¼l milk

1 teaspoon vanilla essence

2 eggs

Preheat the oven to 180°C (350°F) fan bake. Grease 6 small individual ovenproof dishes.

To make the caramel, place 80g of the sugar in a saucepan and dissolve with a little water. Cook over a high heat for a few minutes, until bubbles form and the caramel turns a dark brown. Pour into the prepared dishes.

Soak the sultanas in hot water for 10 minutes. Place the rice in a saucepan with the milk. Cook over a low heat, stirring regularly, for 30 minutes or until the rice is tender and the milk has been absorbed. Mix in the vanilla essence and the drained sultanas. Beat in the eggs and the remaining sugar.

Divide among the prepared dishes. Bake for 30 minutes and serve warm, as the pudding will become drier as it cools.

# Dried apricot and polenta triangles

*Serves 6*

In this recipe, the dried apricots benefit from being soaked in hot water. This makes them more moist, and it is easier to cut the mixture into triangles.

10 dried apricots

150g polenta

600ml milk

55g sugar

zest of 1 lemon

30g butter

Pour boiling water over the apricots and soak for 10 minutes. Place the polenta and milk in a saucepan and bring to the boil. Add the sugar and finely grated zest of the lemon, and stir for 5 minutes until thick. Drain and finely chop the dried apricots, and mix into the polenta. Remove from the heat and leave to cool, covered, for 15 minutes.

Line a 27 × 18cm (11 × 7 inch) baking tin with cling film and pour the polenta on top. Level the surface and chill until firm. Cut into portions to make 18 triangles.

Melt the butter in a frying pan and cook each triangle for a couple of minutes on each side, until crispy and golden. Serve with some custard, if desired.

# Dried fruit filo stacks

*Serves 4*

This dessert is light and crunchy, and more importantly tastes delicious. It is also pretty to look at and makes a nice dessert to serve at a dinner party.

5 sheets filo pastry

1 egg yolk

1 tablespoon milk

8 dried apricots

8 pitted prunes

8 stoned dates

8 dried figs

15g butter

2 tablespoons sugar

pinch of ground mixed spice

1 teaspoon vanilla essence

4 tablespoons natural Greek-style yoghurt

Preheat the oven to 180°C (350°F) fan bake. Grease an ovenproof tray.

Stack the sheets of filo pastry and cut into 4 strips along the shortest side. Cut each strip into 3 pieces. Place these 12 pieces of pastry on the prepared tray. Mix the egg yolk with the milk, and use to brush the top of each piece of filo pastry. Bake for 5 minutes or until crispy and golden.

Cut up the apricots, prunes, dates and figs into small pieces. Place in a frying pan with the butter, sugar and mixed spice. Cook over a medium heat for 10 minutes until the fruit is tender, stirring occasionally. Mix in the vanilla essence.

Place 4 pieces of the prepared filo pastry onto 4 dessert plates. Divide the fruit into 3 portions and use 1 portion to cover the pieces of baked pastry. Top with a second piece of pastry and cover with the second amount of fruit. Cover with the remaining pieces of pastry. Use the third amount of fruit to garnish and serve immediately with a dollop of natural Greek-style yoghurt.

# Nuts

Walnut and honey
filo pastries

Coconut
slices

Date and
walnut loaf

Pistachio
shortbreads

Coconut
roly-poly cake

Nuts such as walnuts, pistachios, coconut and almonds can be eaten raw as a snack, or used as a wonderful addition to many recipes, from salads to baked items. They have great nutritional value, containing significant amounts of vitamin E, manganese and omega-3 fatty acids.

Nuts that are still in their shells have the longest shelf life, so shell nuts as and when you need them, as they will taste fresher. To stop shelled nuts from becoming rancid, store them in an airtight container in a cool, dry place away from direct sunlight.

For a roasted flavour and crispy texture, dry-roast nuts and sprinkle them onto desserts and salads. Nuts can be ground or chopped in a food processor — a quick, though noisy, operation!

Walnuts are often used in baking; however, they can also be used in savoury dips, stuffings, and salads, and go very well with cheese. Coconut is different from other nuts, both in size and texture. Its white flesh may be used fresh or dried, while the coconut water contained in the nut provides a refreshing drink. Desiccated coconut is a low-cost ingredient that is commonly used in baking. Salted, roasted pistachios are another popular snack food. Fresh, unsalted pistachios add an unusual flavour to baked goods, ice creams and sauces. Something to always bear in mind is that nuts may cause choking, especially in young children, and some nuts are among the most highly allergenic foods.

# Date and walnut loaf

*Serves 6*

This is an ideal afternoon tea treat that I also enjoy having for breakfast. Filling and nutritious, it makes a wonderful snack for children or as an addition to their packed lunch. It will keep for several days in an airtight container.

200g dates

150ml water

80g brown sugar

80g unsalted butter, melted

1 egg

230g flour

1 tablespoon baking powder

70g walnut pieces

Preheat the oven to 180°C (350°F) fan bake. Grease a 23 × 12cm (9 × 5 inch) loaf tin.

Bring the water to the boil. Chop the dates, place in a bowl, and cover with the water. Mix the brown sugar with the melted butter. Beat in the egg. Stir in the flour, the baking powder and the walnut pieces. Add the dates and water, and mix until well combined.

Pour this mixture into the prepared tin and bake for 40 minutes, or until a fine skewer or toothpick inserted into the centre of the cake comes out clean. Cut into slices and serve with a cup of tea or coffee, or with a glass of milk.

# Walnut and honey filo pastries

*Serves 6*

This recipe is inspired by *baklava*, the famous Greek dessert I remember enjoying as soon as we set foot on the Cycladic Islands many years ago. It was packed with chopped walnuts and drizzled with honey and butter. My version is lighter but also uses filo pastry, which is very popular in Greek cuisine.

100g unsalted butter

8 filo pastry sheets

140g walnut pieces

70g brown sugar

Preheat the oven to 180°C (350°F) fan bake. Grease a 35 x 27cm (14 x 11 inch) biscuit tray.

Melt 40g of the butter. Place a sheet of filo pastry on the prepared tray. Lightly brush with the melted butter, and top with another filo pastry sheet. Repeat to use 5 of the filo pastry sheets.

Roughly chop the walnuts and mix with the brown sugar. Melt the remaining butter, set aside 1 spoonful, and mix the rest into the walnuts. Spread the walnut mixture thinly over the filo pastry sheets. Top with the remaining pastry sheets, lightly brushing each one with the reserved butter. Bake for 20 minutes or until crispy and golden. Cut up into 12 slices and serve warm or cold.

# Pistachio shortbreads

*Serves 6*

Pistachios originate from Western Asia. They are said to significantly reduce the risk of heart disease, a characteristic they share with other nuts, making them a guilt-free and heart-friendly snack.

Preheat the oven to 180°C (350°F) fan bake. Grease a 35 x 27cm (14 x 11 inch) biscuit tray.

To make the pistachio shortbreads, combine the melted butter with the icing sugar and mix until smooth. Roughly chop the pistachios in a food processor and add to the mixture. Lastly, beat in the flour and mix to a crumbly consistency.

Spread into the biscuit tray in a layer, 3mm thick. Bake for 15 minutes or until slightly golden. Remove from the oven and immediately cut rounds out of the baked shortbread mixture. Place the pistachio shortbreads on a plate, and leave to cool.

To make the pistachio cream, whip the cream until firm. Be sure to use very cold cream to do this, as it makes this step much easier. Set aside. Beat the egg yolk with the icing sugar in a mixing bowl. Add the softened cream cheese and finely ground pistachios. Mix until smooth. Lastly, fold in the whipped cream carefully. Refrigerate for 1 hour.

Assemble by piping a spoonful of pistachio cream onto each shortbread. Garnish with the roughly chopped pistachios and accompany with a cup of tea.

## Pistachio shortbreads

125g unsalted butter, melted

70g icing sugar

100g pistachios

175g flour

## Pistachio cream

150ml fresh cream

1 egg yolk

55g icing sugar

100g cream cheese

55g pistachios, finely ground

30g pistachios, roughly chopped, to garnish

# Coconut slices

*Makes 18*

These coconut slices will appeal to children, and make a great afternoon snack. Let your children dip them in chocolate for maximum fun.

2 eggs

150g sugar

1 teaspoon vanilla essence

150g desiccated coconut

70g oat bran

1 apple

30g dark chocolate

2 tablespoons water

Preheat the oven to 120°C (250°F) fan bake. Grease a 35 × 27cm (14 × 11 inch) biscuit tray.

Beat the eggs, sugar and vanilla essence until pale yellow. Add the desiccated coconut and mix until well combined. Mix in the oat bran. Peel and finely grate the apple and add to the mixture.

Spread this mixture evenly onto the prepared tray. Bake for 15 minutes or until golden, and leave to cool. Cut up into 18 rectangles.

Chop the dark chocolate and melt in the microwave with 2 tablespoons of water. Mix well and dip each coconut slice into the melted chocolate. Chill for 10 minutes or until the chocolate is set.

# Coconut roly-poly cake

*Serves 6*

Roly-poly cake is a favourite among the young and the not-so-young. It can be filled with all sorts of ingredients and flavoured with various liqueurs. In this case, I have used desiccated coconut and coconut milk for the sponge. Your favourite jam, lemon curd or a chocolate spread may be substituted for the apricot jam.

4 eggs, separated

100g sugar

70g flour

55g desiccated coconut

3 tablespoons coconut milk

100g apricot jam

natural yoghurt, for garnish (optional)

Preheat the oven to 180°C (350°F) fan bake. Grease a 35 × 27cm (14 × 11 inch) rectangular baking tin.

To make the sponge, whisk the egg yolks and sugar until light and foamy. Fold in the sifted flour. Add the coconut milk and two-thirds of the desiccated coconut. Beat the egg whites into soft peaks and fold delicately into the batter.

Pour this mixture into the prepared tin. Bake for 10 to 15 minutes or until springy to the touch. Remove from the tin and place on a damp tea towel.

Spread the jam over the sponge, leaving 2cm (1 inch) clear on all sides. Roll up from the short end and chill. Cut 1cm (½ inch) off both ends, and sprinkle with the remaining desiccated coconut. Serve with a dollop of natural yoghurt, if desired.

# Acknowledgements

First of all, I would like to express my heartfelt thanks to Tracey Wogan, non-fiction commissioning editor at HarperCollins NZ, who gave me her support from our first discussion. Many thanks also to my publisher, Lorain Day, and to the rest of the team, in particular Antoinette Sturny and Kate Stone, who helped put this book together. Next, I want to thank my husband for his constant support since I decided to start writing five years ago. He was always there to give me encouragement when I needed it most. Finally, I must thank my lovely children for gracefully taking on the role of guinea pigs when it came to testing my recipes (and for giving me the most honest feedback I could dream of!).

# Biography

Christelle, born in France in 1975, graduated as an electrical and software engineer in 1997. After five years of working in France and the United Kingdom, Christelle and her husband moved to New Zealand, a country that represented everything they were looking for. They settled in Christchurch in 2002, and became New Zealand citizens in 2006.

In 2008, Christelle gave up her day job as a software engineer.

Since then she has been able to fully focus on her four small children and on her new career in food writing. An award-winning author, she is also a food columnist for various publications and produces her own food photography, in addition to keeping fit with daily bike rides and swims.

Ever since she was young, Christelle has taken great pleasure in cooking and baking for her family and friends. She puts her passion for good food down to her mother, whom she thinks is the best cook ever. Christelle loves experimenting in the kitchen, and delights in the art of creating new dishes. Yet her approach to cooking is down-to-earth, and her recipes are easily accessible by the home cook.

Her first book, *Simply Irresistible French Desserts*, was an award-winning collection of her favourite desserts. *French Fare* won an award for Best French Cuisine Cookbook at the Gourmand World Cookbook Awards, while *Passion Chocolat* received an award in the Chocolate category. *Fresh Start – Healthy Recipes and Food Tips for Parents of Preschoolers* received an award for Best Children and Family Cookbook and reflects her role as a mum wanting to give her children a taste for a healthy lifestyle and nutritious foods from an early age. It was translated into several languages. Since then she has published *Self-Publish! A Guide to Publishing Your Own Work* to help other aspiring authors see their work in print.

For more information,
visit Christelle's website
www.christelle-leru.com

# Conversion tables

The following measures have been rounded up or down for convenience and have been kitchen-tested.
The recipe baking times and temperatures are based on the use of a fan oven.

## Metric to imperial

| | | | | |
|---|---|---|---|---|
| 15g | ½ oz | 30ml | 1fl oz | |
| 30g | 1oz | 55ml | 2fl oz | |
| 40g | 1½ oz | 75ml | 3fl oz | |
| 55g | 2oz | 100ml | 3½ fl oz | |
| 70g | 2½ oz | 120ml | 4fl oz | |
| 80g | 3oz | 150ml | 5fl oz | |
| 100g | 3½ oz | 155ml | 5½ fl oz | |
| 125g | 4½ oz | 200ml | 7fl oz | |
| 140g | 5oz | 225ml | 8fl oz | |
| 150g | 5½ oz | 250ml | 9fl oz | |
| 175g | 6oz | 280ml | 10fl oz (½ pint) | |
| 200g | 7oz | 300ml | 10½ fl oz | |
| 210g | 7½ oz | 330ml | 12fl oz | |
| 230g | 8oz | 400ml | 14fl oz | |
| 240g | 8½ oz | 500ml | 18fl oz | |
| 275g | 9½ oz | 555ml | 20fl oz (1 pint) | |
| 300g | 10½ oz | 600ml | 22fl oz | |
| 320g | 11oz | 750ml | 27fl oz | |
| 350g | 12oz | 1 litre | 34fl oz (1¾ pints) | |
| 360g | 12½ oz | 1¼ litre | 2¼ pints | |
| 375g | 13oz | 1½ litre | 2½ pints | |
| 400g | 14oz | 2 litres | 3¼ pints | |
| 410g | 14½ oz | | | |
| 450g | 1lb | | | |
| 500g | 1lb 2oz | | | |
| 600g | 1lb 5oz | | | |
| 700g | 1lb 8oz | | | |
| 750g | 1lb 10oz | | | |
| 800g | 1lb 12oz | | | |
| 1kg | 2lb 3oz | | | |

## Oven temperatures

| | | |
|---|---|---|
| 120°C | 250°F | Gas mark 1 |
| 150°C | 300°F | Gas mark 2 |
| 160°C | 325°F | Gas mark 3 |
| 180°C | 350°F | Gas mark 4 |
| 190°C | 375°F | Gas mark 5 |
| 200°C | 400°F | Gas mark 6 |
| 220°C | 425°F | Gas mark 7 |

## Baking tins

| | | |
|---|---|---|
| Loaf | 23 x 12cm | (9 x 5 inch) |
| Round | 20cm | (8 inch) |
| | 23cm | (9 inch) |
| Rectangular | 27 x 18cm | (11 x 7 inch) |
| Biscuit tray | 35 x 27cm | (14 x 11 inch) |

## Oven dishes

| | | |
|---|---|---|
| Square | 20 x 20cm | (8 x 8 inch) |
| Rectangular | 30 x 18cm | (12 x 7 inch) |
| | 35 x 27cm | (14 x 11 inch) |

## Cups to metric and imperial

| | 1 cup | ½ cup | ¼ cup |
|---|---|---|---|
| Flour | 125g / 4½ oz | 55g / 2oz | 30g / 1oz |
| Sugar | 150g / 5½ oz | 80g / 3oz | 40g / 1½ oz |
| Desiccated coconut | 80g / 3oz | 40g / 1½ oz | 20g / ¾ oz |
| Ground almonds | 100g / 3½ oz | 55g / 2oz | 30g / 1oz |
| Walnut pieces | 80g / 3oz | 40g / 1½ oz | 20g / ¾ oz |
| Yoghurt | 200g / 7oz | 100g / 3½ oz | 55g / 2oz |
| Milk | 250ml / 8½ fl oz | 120ml / 4fl oz | 55ml / 2fl oz |
| Fresh cream | 250ml / 8½ fl oz | 120ml / 4fl oz | 55ml / 2fl oz |
| Water | 250ml / 8½ fl oz | 120ml / 4fl oz | 55ml / 2fl oz |

# Index